OVERCOMING ASPERGER'S
Personal Experience & Insight

written by
Robert S. Sanders, Jr.
© 2002

with Foreword by
Murphy M. Thomas, Ph.D.

October, 2002
To the TTU Library,
with best wishes,
Robert S. Sanders, Jr.
(TTU alumnus 1991)

This important book, with the intent of helping others, is an anecdotal overview portraying the life of a person afflicted with Asperger's Syndrome, a high functioning and mild form of autism. The author, who had autistic traits as a child, has successfully overcome numerous obstacles to lead a reasonably normal life. He holds a degree in Electrical Engineering, and he has occupied himself with construction projects, carpentry and painting. He is now an author and has written several books, among them three science fiction novels, and a novel about an American in Mexico. He travels extensively and enjoys bicycling and hiking.

Various experiences of his life are presented from childhood to the present, and most of them bear certain qualities and characteristics of Asperger's Syndrome. Other important topics and difficulties related to autism are discussed, such as: childhood idiosyncrasies, obsessions and worries, dwelling on subjects, strong convictions, expecting friendships to continue, collecting things, plus other subjects and ideas. There are several anecdotes that point out some bizarre incidents in his life, along with stories that reveal some of the unique and important projects he has accomplished.

Also discussed are possible causes of autism, whether they be from genetic inheritance, out of balance brain chemistries, or even from heavy metals. Some unique and original solutions including insights are also covered. Overcoming Asperger's is all a process as we explore new ideas and concepts.

Overcoming Asperger's: Personal Experience & Insight

Foreword by
Murphy M. Thomas, Ph.D.

proofread and edited by
Martin A. Enticknap

color cover illustration created by
Martin A. Enticknap
copyright © May 2002 by Martin A. Enticknap

cover design by: Brian Matthews
Jobsoft Design and Development Inc.
Murfreesboro, Tennessee

Library of Congress Control Number: 2002109045

ISBN: 1-928798-05-5

type: Non Fiction

Armstrong Valley Publishing Company
P.O. Box 1275
Murfreesboro, TN 37133-1275
Phone: 615-895-5445
Fax: 615-893-2688

printed in the United States of America

TABLE OF CONTENTS

Acknowledgement goes to my parents who raised me and who have inspired me to write this book about Asperger's Syndrome and autism. They have cared about me and my well being, and I appreciate their support in various ways, including their resources of knowledge for use in this compilation. Thanks to their love and support, I have had the time and inspiration to write several novels and now this book.

Acknowledgement goes to Murphy M. Thomas, Ph.D. for the excellent and impressive Foreword that he wrote for this book. I am also grateful to him for his psychological counseling and advice to my parents and me during my early childhood.

Acknowledgement also goes to Martin A. Enticknap for his computer generated cover image artwork for this book, for his numerous conversations with me pertaining to philosophy and human characteristics, and for his proofreading this manuscript, including his ideas and input, some of which I have included in this epistle.

cover image: artist's interpretation:

Hi Robert,
  Well, here is your cover.
  The idea behind the pic is that you are in your castle, calm waters around you. There is a barrier between the world, the city on the right and the forest on the left, but your light shines a way to overcome the barrier, like car lights as you drive out to meet the world on your terms. The light your perspective shines across the water is to invite the reader into your world and out back into theirs, changed and challenged by the journey. The subject of the book is not that easy to convey, but this is my interpretation of your journey. I like the colours, includes a calm mellow orange, which is your favorite colour if I remember correctly.
All the best.
Your friend,
Martin

two photos on back cover:

The author, 1968: Robert Sanders in the kitchen, playing with two Western Electric rotary dial phones. Even early in life, he showed the desire to communicate.

The author, recent: Robert Sanders as an adult.

FOREWORD BY:
Murphy M. Thomas, Ph.D.

I feel greatly honored to write this Foreword for Robert Sanders' book: *Overcoming Asperger's: Personal Experience & Insight*. Back a generation ago in the early 1970's, Robert's parents brought him to me several times for consultation. They were very concerned for him because he was nonverbal in Kindergarten and displayed a variety of aberrant behavior patterns. His first attempt at 1st grade was a disaster. At the time, I was working with the Rutherford County Guidance Center. Robert was transferred to a different school, and thanks to the cooperation of his new teachers who allowed us to monitor his behavior, things greatly improved, and he became much better adjusted. In consideration of Robert's behavior and characteristics during his childhood, he would have been diagnosed (in today's terminology) with Asperger's Syndrome.

This non-fiction book, like Robert Sanders' books of fiction, is about a journey, a trip or a saga. While his novels are about his treks to Mexico, Australia, the British Isles, to points in the American landscape, or even to outer space, *Overcoming Asperger's* is a book that recounts Robert's journey to *inner* space. He describes a phenomenological geography, the valleys of hurt, rejection, despair, and the peeks of hope. This is a book about courage, about single-minded determination and persistence. It is about blazing personal paths, while being guided only by a clear sense of right and wrong. This is a book about integrity.

The term "Asperger's" in the title may deceive one to believe that this journey will take us to strange places, to a foreign land of autistic preoccupations. Instead, this narrative is about the commonplace, yet it describes a heroic figure on a quest to connect and communicate, to become fully human. Robert's struggles are our struggles. We all seek to understand ourselves and connect with others. We all seek to be understood and to be valued. We all strive to live a productive, meaningful and moral life. Through the lens of Asperger's, Robert seems to have a sharper focus on what is essential, and a keener sense of what is right and wrong. He is guided, or compelled, to follow an impeccable path. We pay psychotherapists thousands of dollars to gain such vision and courage. Yet, Robert's exquisite sensitivities cut both ways; and he reminds us of the pain, disappointment and tragedy that exist in all of our lives.

Overcoming Asperger's is a <u>must read</u> for mental health and teaching "professionals." You will laugh, you will cry. If you are honest, you will see yourself, and the limitations (even dangers) of what we do. You will see our personal and professional foibles, and what we need to learn. You will be humbled, brought back to earth, less arrogant. You will no longer be able to smugly diagnose, medicate, educate or modify symptoms. You will be inspired to listen with more respect, to trust in and join with others (our clients, their families, and the caring community), and to appreciate the complexity and paradoxical nature of the human condition.

Also, this is a <u>must read</u> for family, friends, neighbors, even bus drivers, shop keepers - for all of us who are perplexed by or fear diversity. In a simple but elegant way, Robert opens a window for us to appreciate what is so difficult to understand. In his stories, we will recognize our prejudices, how we define people in terms of their differences rather than their strengths, how we hurt others, how ignorance breeds fear and estrangement; yet his accounts reveal how *similar* we are to those whom we distance as being different, and how those with unusual perspectives and standards can challenge and enrich our lives. In a poignant but non-judgmental way, Robert helps us see the best and the worst qualities of the human spirit. In the process, Robert reminds us of the value of community, the importance of acceptance, and the power of love.

This is an inspiring and delightful book. It is filled with hope and good cheer. It is naively straightforward and honest. It cuts to the heart. While this is a book about "overcoming," it is primarily a testament to the power of parental love, the value of friendships, the importance of community, and to the innate strength and wisdom of those who we have labeled as handicapped.

Murphy M. Thomas, Ph.D.
clinical and consulting psychologist
Murfreesboro, Tennessee
August 2002

A NOTE FROM MY FATHER

Robert was a healthy, pleasant, responsive, affectionate toddler until, at age 2½, he drifted away from us, into the shell of apparent autism.

He regressed into being essentially nonverbal, moderately unresponsive, and untouchable. He was a head banger, cried at certain noises (jet airplanes, big trucks, the one-and-only barber shop haircut). We were puzzled and alarmed. His growth and development seemed otherwise normal. He was curious, tirelessly worked jigsaw puzzles, and he rode his rocking horse for long periods, while looking straight through you.

Evaluations by audiologists and my colleagues in pediatrics, psychology, and psychiatry suggested he was "too bright and too well coordinated" to be autistic. His disorder was labeled "adjustment reaction to childhood." This was 25 years before the high functioning section of the autism spectrum (Asperger's Syndrome) was a recognized entity.

We were indeed fortunate that a new psychologist, Murphy M. Thomas, Ph.D., moved to Murfreesboro. He and the Rutherford County Guidance Center, along with a behavior modification team from MTSU, intervened during Robert's second year of Kindergarten. Dr. Thomas guided him in and out of an initial and difficult 1st grade and structured his transfer into another public school with a special education program and kind, caring teachers who were helpful, patient and cooperative.

Robert made great strides in the 3rd grade, thanks to the expertise of another kind and very competent teacher. He became an excellent student, graduating from high school as Salutatorian, with awards in Spanish, Electronics, Geometry, Advanced Math, and the 4.0 Science Award. He received a presidential work scholarship to Tennessee Technological University, and he graduated with a degree in Electrical Engineering.

In this book, Robert graphically describes his life, his accomplishments, and his struggles with negotiations, interpersonal relationships, and making friends.

Robert lives in a separate house on our farm in middle Tennessee. He is a writer, carpenter, painter, and an intrepid traveller. He is a collector of rocks, fossils, books, telephones, station wagons, and a variety of trees and wildflowers. His journals and splendid photographs attest to his reverence for nature and the wilderness.

In more recent years, he has collected (as gifts) bicycles, used appliances, kitchen sinks, computers, and lumber to take to Mexico. We sometimes call him the "Gringo Santa."

Despite his many strengths, the norms of socialization, conformity, and empathy have continued to be difficult for him and puzzling for us. He has ongoing sensory overload episodes, and at times he has been obsessed with the compulsion of completing projects. The latter has been as asset, especially in compiling genealogies and 4 family photo albums, each over 100 pages, of which copies were distributed to all members of the family and greatly appreciated. Some fetishes persist, such as using only rotary dial phones in his home, and driving cars only with a manual transmission.

It was not until Robert was 28 that Dr. Oliver Sacks' remarkable article "An Anthropologist on Mars" appeared in the *New Yorker Magazine* (December 1993/January 1994). The similarities to Temple Grandin were striking, a jolt of enlightenment and a reassuring relief to finally better understand Robert's life of feeling "different."

My wife, Pat, and I are very proud of our son. He has indeed overcome so much. We are also obliged to the community of wonderful teachers and counselors who shepherded his school years, and to family and friends who were supportive along the way. We especially appreciate Dr. Murphy M. Thomas for his continuing guidance and for his Foreword in this book.

Robert S. Sanders, MD, FAAP
August 2002

INTRODUCTION

Autism or Asperger's Syndrome (mild autism) is an abnormality, what some would call a brain disorder, that occurs in a significant percentage of the human population, and until recent times, it wasn't paid attention to or even considered. There is no single cause for it. Autism can be defined as the inability to develope normal emotional stability and coordination when associating with others. Many autistics also have abnormal behavior patterns, and some of them are aloof. One could say they have a different set of codes by which they operate, and it is difficult for them to recognize certain social cues, some of them subtle, such as eye movements and body language, most of which we take for granted. This leads to having problems with communication and with relationships in life. However, there are programs with proper social training, and there are solutions that can really help them along and bring many autistics out of their world and more into ours.

Sometimes autism is inherited and in those cases it is genetic. Other times, it is caused by out of balance brain chemistries, food allergies, or yeast buildup, which after analysis (in those cases) may be treated by monitoring food intake, vitamins, and minerals. Heavy metal poisoning, such as lead, mercury, aluminum, arsenic, cadmium, and thallium can also cause autism. Intravenous and oral types of chelation therapy are good for removing heavy metal toxins.

My autistic traits occurred during my early childhood. As I grew up, most of my autistic traits fell by the wayside. However, some residual characteristics stayed with me: my sensitivities to sounds, perfumes, camera flashes, and smoke, and my sometimes being naive.

Making friends was never all that difficult, but for some of them, keeping those friendships was seemingly a feat beyond my capabilities. While easy for some, it has been difficult at times for me to know how to read and recognize a true friendship. For example, many autistics don't have the instincts to perceive or realize when the other person is tiring or becoming bored, and that the friendship is wearing out or deteriorating. They don't always understand the social expectations of the other person.

On the other hand, making and keeping friends is made more difficult because autism and Asperger's Syndrome are conditions that are not very well understood by many people out there in the general public. To them, autism is like a void or vacuum, and people's worst fears tend to fill that void instead of their understanding and compassion. For my traits, some people are afraid to associate with me. They shy away from autistics and Asperger's because they don't understand them. They are afraid of them and can't figure them out. This book helps to give a human face or might we say a frame of reference to the characteristics of autistics and Asperger's, in hopes that those people who are fearful might become more understanding and accepting.

Nevertheless, there are some friends who I have gotten along fine with. They have stayed my friends, bless their souls, and I appreciate them. My friendships with them are success stories.

During my adolescence as I grew up, I had what would be considered Asperger's Syndrome, the mild form of autism, which is also called high functioning autism. I never saw myself as handicapped, and I believe that was to my benefit. Asperger's Syndrome is not an illness. It is merely a different template for living. Those who have Asperger's also have a different set of codes to work with, and they adapt themselves to life's situations. They have a different way of approaching things, and one might say they take a different and sometimes more difficult road to arrive at the same destination. However, it is not so easily done as a person who is . . . normal. Many people afflicted with Asperger's think literally, linearly, and in one track manners. They have to manually learn the social cues. They have to round off the rougher edges of their sometimes intense, stubborn, and pragmatic characteristics to be more acceptable in society. Many of them have adapted very well and are very successful. Asperger's are not to be loathed nor avoided, even though they might not have the best social skills and behavior. Most of them are good decent people with a lot to offer. Many of them are very thorough and exacting, and they have phenomenal memories. They are persistent and meticulous, which are advantageous for accomplishing tasks, plus other good traits.

I have pretty much overcome Asperger's. However, I still have some lingering high functioning traits to this day. It's really easy for me to remember phone numbers. That trait is a welcome convenience to my life. I resist change. I still have the first car I ever bought, and the subsequent ones, as well. I am persistent, and I am thorough, which I consider an advantage rather than a disadvantage, because with those traits, my stubbornness has caused me to get projects completed, make good grades in school, solve problems, and accomplish many tasks which other people have openly admitted they wouldn't have even considered taking on.

Granted this is not true for all Asperger's, because there are some of them who cannot get things organized, and they don't have the motivation to solve problems and accomplish projects, even though they're highly intelligent. There are many types of Asperger's, and each case is unique in its own way.

Fortunately, in my case, the autism is mild enough that I still have a sense of competence to lead a mostly normal life. Even though I sometimes take things more literally than others, I am clear headed and understand many concepts.

I consider this book an important addition to the personal libraries of psychologists, psychiatrists, teachers in training, and teachers.

Some of the topics in this book are my viewpoints and may be considered my opinion about how I interpret the way certain things are. They are not necessarily the opinions of the readers, clinicians, or Ph.D.'s reading this book. What is most important is that yes, it is possible to overcome mild autism and Asperger's Syndrome and enjoy a reasonably normal life.

For those of you who like to read and wish to do a more in-depth study of some of my life's experiences, you may obtain and read my previous novel, *Walking Between Worlds*, a novel of an American in Mexico, written by my pen name, Robert Alquzok, length 400 pages, ISBN 1-928798-02-0. I consider my previous novel a companion book to this one. The hero of the novel is Roland Jocelyn, a young American fellow who makes repeated trips to a small quaint town called Bustamante, Nuevo León. He enjoys adventures, experiences some good friendships, but he also experiences conflicts, misunderstandings, and scandals. Roland's experiences are a take off of me and my different adventures in Mexico during a 10-year period. With the recent influx of Mexicans into American society, this important novel portrays an example of Mexican-American relations and culture. *Walking Between Worlds* is on print-on-demand status with Ingram Book Company and is always available for order from any bookstore. Plus I also have on hand copies for sale.

It is my hope that you will enjoy the following topics, anecdotes, and personal experiences throughout this book and that they will help you gain insights and a better understanding of the life of a high functioning Asperger's.

Robert Sanders with his parents and grandparents.
December 1965

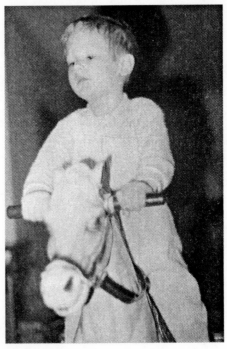

Robert Sanders on "Clip Clop", 1968

PART 1

ADOLESCENT DEVELOPMENT

Preschool Childhood

I only have a handful of memories before age 4 and a few more from age 4 to 5. I have my first memories of being at my grandparents' house in Crossville, one of being inside at the dining room table, and another of playing in the yard with a woman named Marjorie. We played around a Spruce tree.

Mother used to give me puzzles to work with and solve. Those were very helpful in increasing my intelligence, mental capacity, and mental clarity. Brain development is very important, especially during the first few years of life. I remember the playpen outside where I used to play and run around. I also spent some of my time rocking on a rocking horse called "Clip Clop."

I remember my first feelings of sensitivity when I was three. Back in those days, the late 1960's, nearby Smyrna's Sewart Air Force Base was in use, and jets used to fly overhead at times, either on their way to Arnold Engineering Development Center in Tullahoma, Tennessee, or to Huntsville, Alabama and the multitude of military bases there. They sometimes flew closely overhead. One time when I was in the back garden, one of them roared overhead with its shrill sounds, which scared me. I ran back into the house crying. (Perhaps that would have scared any child of 3 years old!)

During my early childhood, I had significant autistic traits. I had only a 25-word verbal vocabulary at age 3, and most of that was baby talk. I didn't talk much, and my parents realized that I was having developmental delays. They were concerned about me and thought perhaps I had hearing problems. They took me to a lady doctor named Ann Sitton at the Bill Wilkerson Center in Nashville to have my hearing tested. I actually remember waiting in the waiting room and undergoing the test. My hearing tested excellent. Plus, she estimated that I had a 1,500 word vocabulary of understanding.

My parents asked the doctor if I might be autistic, and she commented that she didn't think so. Autistic people were supposed to be retarded and severely impaired. She told them that it was psychological and that I was quiet for my "elected mutism." That is how I was first diagnosed, based on the general lack of information about autism in those days.

Still, I had the yearning desire to communicate. The photo of me at age 3 on the back of this book portrays that. I don't believe I was "elected mutism" as they labeled me as much as I wasn't yet sure how to piece the words together at such a young age.

By the time I was 4, I finally started talking in complete sentences. The same was true with my father's father, when he one day surprised his mother with complete sentences at age 4. He was good with math like I am, along with other traits, as well. However, he had one trait that I don't have. He had a photographic memory and could memorize page after page of text, something I can't do. On the other hand, I am good at remembering events during my life, and especially at remembering numbers and names.

When I was nearly 4, my parents added a back porch to the house. It was a major change that frustrated me, and I was head banging to release frustration. Sometimes, my head got bruised, and sometimes I broke windowpanes. One day when I was already 5, I broke a windowpane and cut my forehead, and that ended my hand banging episodes.

In my early childhood, I felt really alien to the culture here, like maybe I was from a faraway star system. For those who believe in reincarnation, maybe this is my very first lifetime on Earth, while other humans alive here today may be living their 10th, 100th, or even higher number lifetime. They've had plenty of experience, but since I'm living my first Earth human lifetime, I've had no prior experience. Therefore, I behaved very strangely in early childhood, but finally got the hang of it by age 9 or 10 and became at least somewhat more normal.

In other words, I would say that in my case of overcoming my autistic traits, I learned step by step, detail by detail (what others seem to know almost by instinct) the mannerisms of how to be a person and how to grow up during childhood.

I state the above speculation about my childhood to point out that there is a lot out there that we humans don't know. While my reasons for my abnormalities in early childhood likely stemmed from autism, perhaps they also stemmed from living my first? life on Earth, one or both.

As to reincarnation, I had a few strange experiences in early childhood to realize and believe that we humans have a life force, a spirit or soul that keeps us animated. I also believe the spirit is detachable and that each spirit has its own intelligence for each human alive on Earth. So, why can't that same spirit after its body's death return to Earth for another lifetime, and again, and again?

The reader may refer to the Appendix where I discuss several important topics, including brain development, thoughts outside the brain, reincarnation, and the healing power of the mind.

Diagnosis . . . Accurate or Catch-All?

This is an appropriate place to mention diagnosis since preschool childhood is the age group when most of the people with some form of autism are diagnosed. While doctors, clinicians, and physicians go about the processes of diagnosing thousands of people per year, they need to keep an open mind to alternative possibilities, even if some of them exist outside their realm of beliefs, for one, reincarnation, which many people are adamantly against believing. People act the way they do for a multitude of factors and reasons, and misdiagnoses will be kept to a minimum if those doing the diagnosing keep open minds and consider various possibilities and causes for the "disorder."

Please note that it is important not to make overuse of clinical diagnoses of people thought to have Asperger's Syndrome. There are a lot of people out there who have very high IQ's, so it must be kept in mind that not all of them are "high functioning autistics." Excessive use of diagnoses can even lead to misdiagnoses.

In my case, for the childhood traits I had, I admit that I had what clinicians would now call "Asperger's Syndrome." However, I must also admit that I sometimes have the feeling that the "Asperger's Syndrome" label has or is becoming a quick and easy catch-all label, or a convenient excuse to explain adult idiosyncrasies or childlike behavior in highly intelligent, otherwise normal adults.

More and more children are being diagnosed with autism or Asperger's Syndrome each year, partly due to better testing and awareness and knowing more about how to recognize the condition. The number of cases are rising. I personally believe that there may be other reasons, to do with new souls. The reader may refer to the topic, *Reincarnation? Inexperienced Souls?* in the Appendix to read more about that.

Kindergarten

I remember my first day of Kindergarten in 1970. In those days there was no public Kindergarten, and I was placed at the First Methodist Church Kindergarten program with a Mrs. Johnson. My father took me to school each day, and he worked diagonally across the street.

My father walked me to the door of the classroom, and I didn't like the idea of being left alone with strangers and away from my home and family. Two years earlier, I had been to a Sunday school session in that same room, and I cried the whole period by the door, wanting to leave.

Kindergarten class seemed so alien to me. I didn't know what to make of it. It was a change from my routine. I immediately lay down on the floor. As far as talking, I suddenly didn't feel right. I felt an alien barrier, a mental block, and though I wanted to talk, I just couldn't bring myself to do it. It was too difficult and embarrassing. What was I going to do? I felt in despair, trapped in a way.

Well, I eventually got used to being there, but in subtle protest, there were a couple of things I just refused to do. One of them was talking. I would not talk in the class, nor in the building, and not even in the playground. It's as if it was prohibited for me to talk . . . while attending school. I only forgot and slipped up twice, briefly saying something to two different classmates.

The other significant idiosyncrasy was that I refused to swallow my saliva, and every day it would build up in my mouth. Several times a day, when it got to an annoying level, I would enter the classroom bathroom, pull a paper towel out of the dispenser, and release the whole mouthful of spit and saliva into it, simultaneously dropping it into the trash can. Embarrassing traits, especially the latter, as I look back on it, but then since I didn't talk, I therefore didn't have to swallow, I reasoned.

Another classmate, Tommy, and his family would pray for me each night at their home. Even still, the barrier and problem was not overcome for another year.

Now, mind you, there were a few of those classmates who came out to play with me on the farm. Of course, my parents were the ones who set all that up. Weren't those classmates surprised when I suddenly talked to them as soon as we left the church/school and got in the car! I talked to them at home, as well. One of them, Ricky, later played with me and talked to me at school, but there I wouldn't talk to him. Another classmate who came out to play was Michael.

Anyway, the year went by, and they never got me to talking. So, guess what? I flunked Kindergarten! Well, a more appropriate term is to say that I was held back.

My second year of Kindergarten was at the same church, and that year, I had a Mrs. McKnight. She was a good teacher who cared about us, and she motivated us and saw it as important that we always complete whatever projects we started. She is likely part of the reason why I have the drive to succeed and that I take on and complete projects, even to this day.

I liked the classmates better than the year before. They weren't quite as big, but then I was a year older and therefore bigger myself. Still, I wouldn't talk, but at least I learned how to swallow. I abolished that restriction myself. There was one classmate I became good friends with. His name was Jody, and we played in the playground.

Jody repeatedly came out to visit on the farm and even spent the night during some weekends. He, of course, noticed that I talked at home, and this one was persistent in asking me why I couldn't also talk at school? Finally, in February, well into the school year, Mrs. McKnight and the whole class gathered around me and repeatedly urged me to talk. Finally I did, but in a wrong voice, and I wasn't able to use the right one. But I did talk, an improvement indeed.

Now, to add to the complexity, I would not talk in my right voice while I had on my school clothes, even though they were not dress clothes, nor were they uniforms. Each day when I got out of school and mother picked me up, I would change into a shirt with a number and at that time would be able to use my right voice. It's as if during my early school years I was living a dual existence or a dual personality. One might say that there was possibly an "extra entity" in my psyche that finally exited when I got to 3rd grade, the time that I did away with my wrong voice.

Much of my childhood I remember very well, and I enjoyed making a few friends during my two years of Kindergarten. Jody and I were good friends right through 9th grade, and I still call and talk with him on occasion.

One can realize that I had significant trouble adjusting to change and going to school. A change in routine was not my choice in those days. I had very stubborn traits and purposefully placed excruciating restrictions upon myself, which I wanted to get out of, once I placed them, but I couldn't. I am grateful to Mrs. McKnight and to my classmates for caring enough about me and working with me to finally get me to talk.

10023

Between Kindergarten and 1st grade, I became interested in numbers. Perhaps seeing "Sesame Street" on TV nearly every afternoon got me interested. I knew a little bit about numbers, and I knew how to count to 199. One morning I asked my father what number came after 199. He told me "200."

Oh, of course! I realized. The next number was 201, and it wasn't long before I realized that one hundred numbers after 200 was 300, then 400, 500, 600, 700, and so on. He explained that 10 hundred is exactly 1 thousand, but I stayed with the "hundred" naming, realizing up through 99 hundred. The number after 9999 was 10 thousand (10,000) my father explained. The next digit was 100 thousand, then 1 million, then 1 billion, 1 trillion, 1 quadrillion, and so on!

Mother took me to some summer program one day in Nashville with a Rita Chris, and I remember counting out loud and silently to as much as 5,000. I was so enthralled with numbers that I took on a major project when I was 6 years and 11 months. I used my mother's Royal manual typewriter and typed every number from 1 to 10,000. Each day I would put in time on it, in addition to riding my new bike around the farm and playing with Jody when he would come to visit.

It took about three weeks for me to do it, but I had the stubbornness and persistence to stay with the task, and I finally reached 10,000. It amounted to around 25 pages full of numbers. I certainly had a clear understanding of numbers after that and how many there were! When I reached 10,000, I was so into it that I didn't exactly stop. I went on just a little bit further, stopping at 10,023.

I had those pages of text for several months, perhaps a year, and then they were never seen again . . . mysteriously lost.

One must realize that it is very rare for a 6 or 7 year old to type clear to 10,000, well, that is 10,023.

Speedometers and Odometers

While I'm talking about numbers, I will mention that I always used to keep up with the mileage on my parents' cars. Our 1970 Volvo had a speedometer/odometer that went to a million. It also had a smaller odometer that could be punched to zero whenever one liked. It went to a thousand. By the summer of 1974, our car already reached 100,000, and since it didn't register tenths of a mile, and the smaller one did, I decided to punch it to zero exactly when the car reached 100,000. Several times, my parents forgot and punched it to zero, and I got upset at that because it was no longer synchronized with the main odometer, and I would have to wait until it would reach another thousand, and be lucky enough to be present and *remember* to press it at the exact moment! After numerous thousands of miles, I finally got it right, and convinced my parents that I wanted the smaller odometer left alone. My parents were never as exacting, like I was and still am to some degree.

I kept speedometer/odometers on all my earlier bicycles, and by the time the year 2000 came, I finally had to break away from the tradition, because they weren't being made anymore! Plus, I only wanted analog speedometers driven by a cable, nothing electronic. In the early 1990's I had bought several analog speedometer/odometers to keep in stock for the future, and when I put one of them on my Schwinn 5-speed at the time it reached 10,000 (0000), the replacement speedometer/odometer only reached 279 and stopped turning! So, I put another one on, to discover that the new cables were defective in size!!

Right into my 30's, I was very picky about the mileage on my bicycles. I wanted to be the one to put *all* the miles on that speedometer/odometer, and no one else. One time, only 5 years ago, while in Mexico, I loaned my bicycle to someone for 30 minutes. He put a mile on it. I forgot to disconnect the speedometer cable before letting him ride it. When he returned, right in front of him and others who were with us, I turned my bicycle upside down, turned the front wheel backwards, and took that mile off the speedometer/odometer! There! That made that right. One fellow whose family I was staying with rode my bicycle some 17 or 18 miles, and when I got home, I took a bike ride just that length, with the cable drive mechanism turned around backwards. Made that right again!

I know most people think I'm crazy to do that, but it's my right to be exacting about who puts *all* the 10,000 miles on my own Schwinn bicycle, and I achieved that goal. The speedometer/odometer lasted the whole way through. It was made in 1984, the days when they were still made right.

I refuse to advance (refuse to succumb) to the digital speedometer/odometers, and I therefore no longer clock my miles on my bicycles. The problem I have with digital speedometer/odometers is that as soon as the battery is removed, all the miles are erased, and any battery is going to discharge after a maximum of 10 or 15 years.

1st Grade (Problems and Solutions)

It was the fall of 1972, and the location was Murfreesboro's MTSU Campus School, where I entered 1st grade. While the school was not actually a magnet school in today's terminology, it was a special school in the county schools system, and it was an unsaid precedent that the most elite people of Murfreesboro signed up years ahead of time to send their children to elementary school there. It was *"the thing to do."* The school even had a precious *waiting list.* Campus School in those days was a branch of MTSU, Middle Tennessee State University, and it was set up as a special school for training student teachers.

My parents were led to believe that Campus School would be the ideal school for me, following my troubles in Kindergarten. It was a fine laboratory school that would have good student teachers, complete with behavior modification teams that would enter from time to time and be beneficial to students like me.

I had already been at Mrs. Boutwell's summer enrichment program at the same school 2 months earlier, and I recognized some of the classmates from that.

My teacher was Mrs. Rucker, a 42-year-old Afro-American woman who had served some prestigious positions in town prior to being a teacher. We had some math and reading sessions. I was 7 and still couldn't read, except of course, for numbers. We had workbooks in which we wrote answers, and things went fine for a few weeks, until I didn't fill out a question well enough, and Mrs. Rucker told me, "You don't get a hundred for that!"

One day while walking down the hall in line formation, Mrs. Rucker suddenly came up behind me and spanked me while walking. That made me quite angry! At lunch, I stuck my tongue out at her several times, and she declared, "Don't you dare stick your tongue out at me!"

Things soon deteriorated and Mrs. Rucker gave spankings in addition to slaps on the thigh and other abuse, such as shaking me when I played with the toys! I became more frustrated! I was all over the classroom. I would crawl under desks and tables, and I threw things out the window. As a result, Mrs. Rucker became more abominable! The way she treated me was appalling! She moved my desk out of the classroom and into the hall. I became even more frustrated during my last few days in her class. I squeezed classmates on the back of the neck and got into fights. The mother of one of the students whose neck I had squeezed came to the school and complained.

One day in early November, two months into the school year, Mrs. Rucker called my parents and asked if she could give me a great big paddling! How horrible of her to even think of doing such a thing to me! She had been abominable enough already! My parents quickly told her, "Absolutely not!" Mother was quite irritated at the way Mrs. Rucker had treated me, and she expressed her dissatisfaction. Mrs. Rucker became quite defensive. Her methods stemmed from an old fashioned school of thought, and she wouldn't admit to her incompetency and that she didn't know how to deal with me.

My parents went to the school and were shocked when the school's principal claimed, "We have No children with problems in this school." Therefore they didn't have to deal with special case children, because they "didn't have any." That was a total lie, what with all the problems that I was undergoing, not to mention the mother of one of the students with a sore neck! My parents found out the truth that the school would *not* under any circumstances allow behavior modification teams to enter the school to work with their students. After all, MTSU Campus School was an elitist school.

From the start, my parents had specifically requested the other 1st grade teacher. Campus School's principal was unyielding, and as a means of trying to prove that she knew what was best for each student, she assigned me to Mrs. Rucker on purpose. If my parents had requested Mrs. Rucker, I'm sure the principal would have assigned me to the other one.

(As a side note, that principal was so unyielding that when various teachers had requested air conditioning, she had put her foot down and declared No!)

Now don't get me totally wrong. That other 1st grade teacher wasn't exactly an angel either. One of my friends had her for 1st grade, and on the first day of class, she had every student write the name of the street they lived on. Evidently, she expected them to spell it right because when my friend, who barely knew how to read at the time, spelled it wrong, she "bit his head off," took him to the front of the class, and yelled at him the correct way to spell it!

To add to the mouth of the lions that I was rescued from, 2nd grade would have been a living nightmare, because that teacher's best friend was the paddle! Another friend of mine much later told me that the teacher was a basket case. He was paddled every day in 2nd grade, that is, until his parents went to Campus School irate with the teacher, and they firmly told her that if she paddled her son again, they were going to sue the school! Good on them! I'm glad they threatened that school teacher. They put her in her place. That school ought to be ashamed of itself for all the paddling and abuse it did!

No matter what, Campus School which is "by far the better school" has stayed open and still serves as an elitist school, complete with its fancy *waiting lists*. To this day, the more elite parents sign up their newborns several years ahead of time to go to elementary school there.

One more thing I will add about my memories of 1st grade at Campus School, is that I found one of the other classmates to be cute. I wanted to be friends with him, but I didn't know how to go about doing it. In frustration caused by Mrs. Rucker, and in efforts to be friends with him, I squeezed him on the neck, several times during the 2½ months I was there. I felt bad about having done that to him, and I was sorry I did. I totally failed on my friendship efforts with that classmate. At least I did know him while I was in high school, and of course, we behaved reasonably. I thought about apologizing to him for the neck squeezing of 1st grade, but I decided not to remind him that I was the one who had done it. In other words, I didn't want to open up that can of worms.

As to Campus School, thank goodness my parents took me out of that place! They moved me over to Bellwood Elementary School, where I was well received by the kind principal, Mrs. Baldwin. My mother met with my new teachers. One of them was Mrs. Fran Dean, and she could tell that my mother was quite upset at Campus School and the incompetent way they had handled me.

There was a psychological assessment team that consisted of several special education officials with the Rutherford County Guidance Center. Among the psychologists were Dr. Murphy Thomas and Dr. Jack Schnelle. They were the ones who communicated with the Murfreesboro City Schools office and helped get me placed at Bellwood School, a superior school with resources available that Campus School did not offer! On the Request for Pupil Personnel Services form, they wrote: "child kicked out of Campus School." Dr. Thomas observed that I had problems of adjustment and "displayed a variety of aberrant behavior patterns." That is, my behavior deviated from normal. He kindly wrote a letter to the school superintendent, Mr. Baxter Hobgood, explaining the situation, recommending me to Bellwood, and also offering their continued interest and willingness to work with the school to aid me in my adjustment to normal classroom environments. For the next year and a half, they did a behind-the-scenes monitoring of my behavior and progress. Some members of the team periodically came to Bellwood posing as "teachers in training" to observe the classroom that I was in. The real reason they were there was to observe me. In addition to that, there were Weekly Progress Reports that were filled out by certain officials. Handwritten comments were made in three different sections of those reports: Problem, Treatment, and Progress & Status. They did a fine job and are to be commended for their efforts and their thoroughness, and I am grateful that such services existed back in the early 1970's.

Though I never knew it until I wrote and compiled this book, my parents also had a meeting with both Dr. Thomas and Dr. Schnelle about my disaster at Campus School. They were very worried about me and asked the psychologists if I should be on some sort of *medicine* to get me back on track. Dr. Thomas was very reassuring to my parents that Bellwood was a much better place for me and that he and the other psychologists would be monitoring my behavior behind the scenes. He reckoned that my continued association with other students and making new friends would eventually normalize things. He explained to my parents that he was opposed to the use of anti-psychotic drugs because they were known to most of the time exacerbate problems instead of solve them. I am very grateful to Dr. Thomas. That was a very important decision and turning point in my life. Who knows what might have happened otherwise!

Now that I was in a new school, I had a clean slate. I made the conscious decision that I was never going to be spanked . . . never! I didn't squeeze any more necks, didn't misbehave excessively, and I made some good friends, the normal way. Never ever was I spanked nor paddled for the rest of my whole school career. It's as if I had protection from upstairs from November 1972 forward.

One of my new teachers was Mrs. Boyd, who was a special education teacher, and her class was in a portable double classroom building set apart from the rest of Bellwood School. One might say, in my special case, that Mrs. Boyd was my homeroom teacher, because I spent most of the time in the normal classes with two other teachers, Mrs. Dean and Mrs. Baskin. All of them were fine teachers who cared about me. It was Mrs. Dean who taught me how to read and write, and I had Math with Mrs. Baskin. There was P.E. class with Mr. Hartley. He was also a kind and caring teacher, and he had quite a memory for names. I ran all over the place, and I enjoyed that class. For part of the year, Mr. Hartley had a student teacher named Mr. Bonner.

I made some good friends in 1st grade and I was glad to be away from Campus School. I made sure and behaved myself better and with more self-control, so my new friends wouldn't turn against me.

I will mention a success story pertaining to making friends. Again I picked out someone who I then thought was cute, and this time I made sure I didn't squeeze any necks. I talked to him. He responded, and we quickly became friends. He came out to my house to play, and I went to his house several times. We had a great friendship. I really felt a sense of accomplishment on making friends, and I knew him through the rest of elementary school. I've talked with him a few times in recent years, as well.

(As a side note, 22 years later, 1994, I looked up Mrs. Rucker, and I met with her. I told her what she had done to me back when I had her in first grade. She didn't remember much of it, but she was genuinely upset with herself for what she had done, and she said, "Robert, for all those things I did to you, I'm sorry." I accepted her apology, and she asked me, "Friends?" We shook hands. It was nice to work that out while still alive here on Earth.)

In order to monitor my behavior, Mrs. Boyd sent me to P.E. class with a half sheet of paper so the teacher could rate my condition: Excellent, Very Good, Good, Fair, and Poor. I usually got Goods or Very Goods, but never got Excellents. One day, I decided to hide in the bleachers instead of forming in line with my classmates. Mr. Bonner a few minutes later walked over to me and found me. I thought it was funny. I wasn't punished, but at the end of the P.E. period, he gave me a rating of Poor. Mrs. Boyd asked me why, and I told her that I hid. While she said that wasn't the right thing to do, she was somewhat relieved because what would have been worse is for me to have picked on the other kids. I later asked Mr. Bonner why he never gave me an Excellent, and he said if I would talk to the other classmates, he would give me that rating. So, one day I made sure and behaved very well, and I talked with the other classmates. I achieved an Excellent, and I felt a great sense of accomplishment.

No one knew about my right and wrong voice, and I didn't want my teachers to find out either. One day, Mother took me over to Mrs. Boyd's house. While they talked and visited, discussing my progress, I said nothing. After an hour, we left, and the next day at school, my teacher asked me why I wouldn't talk. I didn't have an answer.

A week or two later, Mother visited Mrs. Boyd again, and I went along. Still, I was quiet, but as we drove away, I decided to wave goodbye and decided to use my right voice to call out, "Goodbye." Mrs. Boyd heard the difference, and first thing the next morning, she asked me what voice I was going to use from now on. I answered, "Right voice," using my normal voice. I was thrilled I could do it, and I ran swiftly to the main building where I had normal class with Mrs. Dean.

Saying that in my right voice was a major breakthrough, or so I thought, because I still couldn't bring myself to use my right voice once I got to Mrs. Dean's class a minute later. Even still, I talked very little to my classmates. Mother, Mrs. Dean, and Mrs. Boyd devised a plan to encourage me to talk. Mother rewarded me a penny a word every time I talked to my classmates. At first, it was just a few words per day, and each afternoon, mother would go by the bank and get pennies from the teller.

As a result, I became interested in coin collecting, and I found lots of wheat pennies. In 1973, wheat pennies were commonplace. I also liked half dollars, and as the days passed by, I started collecting half dollars. After a month, I had $74 worth of half dollars saved up.

Meanwhile, I talked more and more, and the "pay" was good. One day, I racked up 125 words, and Mrs. Dean sent the reported amount to Mrs. Boyd, who complimented me. My parents were pleased and they informed me that I was on my own now, that I would no longer be paid to talk. Of course, they were concerned I might clam up, but I didn't. I continued to talk to my classmates, and I enjoyed knowing them. Still, I used my wrong voice.

As for learning, it was hard for me to learn to read, but Mrs. Dean was a good teacher who was able to cause the students to learn, something Mrs. Rucker was unsuccessful in doing with me. I used to look away a lot during reading sessions, and she was concerned that I wasn't grasping the concepts. Well, she soon got her answer, because I did, thanks to her, learn to read by the end of the year. However, I was at the bottom of the group.

Now, Math was a different story. It was easy, doing addition and subtraction, wanting to know how many of certain objects there were, and other simple problems. No numbers ever went above 99, and it annoyed me why the makers of the 1st grade workbooks thought 1st graders couldn't comprehend 3-digit numbers! Anyway, I spent one early afternoon of my free time in Mrs. Boyd's class and answered the whole rest of the workbook. There! That took care of that boring nuisance! I was very pleased with myself, and Mrs. Boyd was impressed, followed by Mrs. Dean, Mrs. Baskin, and my parents! With that, I proved my intelligence, and when the end of the school year came, I certainly passed and went on to 2nd grade, even though I was slow in reading.

To me, 1st grade seemed like more than a year, since I attended two different schools. I am grateful to my parents for taking me out of MTSU Campus School, placing me in Bellwood Elementary School, and for encouraging me to talk. A lot of students had parents who couldn't have cared less, and they never even came to the school, much less did they meet their children's teachers. Mother always got involved and met all the teachers. She had been a school teacher before she married and saw it as important to know the people who taught her children.

Strong Convictions

One can see that I had strong convictions and placed, as it turned out, unnecessary restrictions on myself early in life. Perhaps this gave me good practice in having strong convictions even now, which is why I have never fallen prey to drugs and alcohol, smoking, premarital sex, or even saying foul language. Early in life, I made a decision I was never going to do those things, and my conscience is so strong, I could never have crossed those lines.

When I was a child, I made some decisions about what I would do or not do through my life. I knew from age 6 forward that I would never smoke, never drink, nor do drugs. I remember my parents saying that when I would be older, say age 12, they would let me try alcoholic beverages. Well, when I was age 8, we were visiting friends in Birmingham, Alabama. I reached for what I thought was a Sprite or Ginger Ale. It was a beer, and what an awful taste it had! I spat it out and washed my mouth out with water. If that's what beer tastes like, why does anyone want it? That became my philosophy, and I saw no need to modify it nor revise it when I reached adolescence. As for whiskey, champagne, wine and the rest of it, one whiff of each of those immediately told me they taste as bad as they smell!

Overcoming Asperger's

When I got to age 12, I knew that since I wasn't going to smoke, drink, or do drugs, I saw no need to try them. What for?

Before I was age 10, I used to eat chocolate like all kids do. Well, I discovered that it made me feel hyper, agitated, and irritable. One day in 4th grade, September 1975, I began to eat a chocolate chip cookie. I put it back in the lunch box. I haven't eaten any chocolate since. There were several tempting moments since then, but I told myself that I no longer eat chocolate. I didn't break my conviction nor revise it. As I now look back on that strong decision I made at age 10, I now realize it was an excellent practice run such that I would never smoke, drink, or do drugs.

I have watched so many teenagers take up smoking, drinking, and the rest of it, and what is really saddening is that some of them have actually told me, when ages 11 and 12, that they would never take up those bad habits. Well, here's how I see it. Where's their memory?! What happened to their convictions? When I was 11 and 12, I told other people I would never smoke, drink, or do drugs. I kept to my word and my convictions. Why haven't those other teenagers kept to theirs? I guess they don't care. They're not as literal as I am, and they don't actually mean what they say.

The issues of staying away from smoking and drinking, revising convictions, and taking up those bad habits, are discussed several times in my novel: *Walking Between Worlds*.

One day when age 12, I remember surprising my aunt and uncle by declaring, "Never!" pertaining to drinking Champagne. My uncle was so surprised, he mentioned it 3 or 4 times to everyone else at the family reunion. I made sure I stayed true to my word as far as drinking, smoking, and doing drugs are concerned . . . *Never*!

For all those teenagers who break their word, it seems like their faces change, and they take on a different look. The look in their eyes changes, also. Some other-level influencing factor (peer pressure and embarrassment) somehow overrides their previous convictions. Their convictions weren't as strong as mine.

If my strong convictions (and NOT revising them) have anything to do with my being an Asperger's, then I am grateful for that in that aspect.

Childhood Idiosyncrasies

There were several childhood idiosyncrasies that I had. One of the main ones, of course already mentioned, was that I didn't talk during my first year of Kindergarten and then later only in my wrong voice until 3rd grade.

Another one was my sensitivity to being touched by others. I didn't like to be touched, as it was not comfortable. This is a common trait among autistics and some Asperger's children. I was 10 years old before I would even shake hands with other people, and only at my parents' urging. Hugging and kissing are things I did even less.

Now, there were a few childhood friends who I gave exemption to my not being touched, and we used to play like normal children. By the time I was a teenager, there were more and more friends who I, without telling them, gave exemptions to, and I for the most part outgrew that idiosyncrasy. However, if a person who I don't like touches me, I still "rub it off."

I was naive when I was ages 5 through 8. I could not relate to certain situations, and I had a lack of understanding of social skills. I was very straightforward and literal. I also couldn't relate to nor understand expressions. Little by little, I grasped and learned the meaning of expressions and understood plenty of abstract concepts.

To point out an example, when I was around 7 years old, I was in the grocery store with Mother, and she was talking with a friend of hers about a young man who accidentally fell down a silo and was miraculously only slightly injured. Falling that distance is usually deadly or can result in serious injuries. Well, Mother told her friend that the young man had a *close call*. I thought, *Close call ... What?* I had no idea why Mother referred to it as a "close call," a common expression I would later learn. What went through my mind was a telephone call occurring in the silo and/or a nearby phone call, and it made no sense to me. Well, maybe the barn had a telephone, for all I knew. The above example points out how literal I was at that age. I'm not as gullible as I used to be, but I do have a tendency to believe a person literally when he/she tells me something.

At times in childhood, I had nervous twitches like looking up every so often or to the side a lot, or sometimes a certain number of times before doing something. It was a tight feeling and compelling urge that was quite annoying to myself and something I wanted to get rid of. Some of these compulsions occurred due to feelings of competition with others, sometimes jealousy, and also general anxiety. I haven't had any nervous twitches since childhood.

From toddler age, my parents had me use a white wooden high chair. I was used to it and continued to use it until I was age 12, at which time I physically outgrew it. It was the chair I was used to, and I didn't want to change to a new and different chair. Of course, I had to when I outgrew it. Now, don't misinterpret how I used the high chair. After age 3 or 4, the tray area that was clamped across the front of the high chair was removed, and I sat in the chair in a more normal fashion, almost like a swivel high stool used in bars or lunch counters.

One classic example of literal interpretation is, say a "friend" doesn't want you coming around, but he's too polite to outright tell you. You ask him if it's okay to continue coming over to visit or chat, and out of his wanting to be polite, he says "yes." That's an answer I still take literally, but the truth of the situation is the person doesn't want me coming over but can't bring himself to tell me. I would view that person's answer of "yes" as a lie, but others, as I have learned over the years, would consider the person "wishy washy" or not straightforward. So, based on *their* viewpoint, the person isn't actually lying.

Other things I had to learn during childhood were how to say "Hi" and "Goodbye" and "See you later" to people. I had to be taught how to answer the telephone. Those things were not natural for me but were learned responses. Perhaps having to be taught those courtesies is normal for everyone, but I have observed even 4 and 5 year olds who seemed to have been *born* with that knowledge and are a natural at it.

Some more idiosyncrasies I had, and this pertained to clothing, was that I did not like belts and never wore them on any pants. I hate ties and I refuse to wear them to this day. I think society is really absurd how they are so picky and how some places of business and even restaurants require them! What's it going to hurt to live your life without a tie and without a belt?! I'm just fine without them. They're useless anyway, especially the tie. Plus, it appalls me how many Asperger's, autistics, and geniuses, even Bill Gates and Einstein, wear/wore ties on a regular basis!

During my early childhood, when in Kindergarten, I wore Farah jeans that had an elastic band, not a belt, and I liked them. By 2nd grade, they were already out of style and were hard to find. I resisted change. Mother managed to find a couple more pairs of larger Farah jeans, and that got me through 3rd grade. Of course, as I continued growing, I was forced to adapt, as Farah jeans became obsolete. I advanced to the Levi's type jeans with a zipper, but I still refused the belt, and to this day, I wear pants without a belt. The only belt I wear is a seatbelt when I'm driving my car or truck or when I'm riding as a passenger.

2nd Grade, Achievement Tests

While I was in 2nd grade, I had a Miss Vance, a strict teacher who was much less enjoyed than my 1st grade teachers at Bellwood. I did not advance in my social skills that whole year. I talked very little in 2nd grade, because the teacher would send to the corner or to the cloakroom anyone who talked. For me, that was counterproductive because I needed to talk more. I remember on the way to lunch one day that one of the students told me, "Say something Robert." Many times when I raised my hand to ask the teacher a question, she snapped, "Put your hand down Robert!" Sometimes I would walk up to her desk to ask her a question, and she almost always barked, "Sit down!" in a rude manner! She was just too strict, very old fashioned in her ways, and she lacked compassion! At least 3rd grade was going to be a lot better.

For the final hour of each class day, I used to go to the portable classroom with Mrs. Boyd, as a means of continued monitoring of my behavior. At least that was some relief to me, to be away from that strict atmosphere!

I also had a speech class with a Judy Beasley. There were only a few of us that had speech problems, and we had our sessions once a week in a Ford Econoline van that she drove to the five different city schools. The letters I had trouble pronouncing were the "s" and the "th" which I corrected without much trouble.

In that year, I did somehow manage to go to the top of my reading group, but where I really did well was in Math. I remember when the achievement tests were given that I even answered several multiplication problems that were *extra* problems that weren't expected of 2nd graders. While taking the test, I figured out a multiplication trick. Instead of performing the normal multiplication procedure, if a 3-digit number was multiplied by 4, for example, I wrote out the 3-digit number 4 times and did long addition. When the time was up, my teacher saw that I had answered those extra problems, and she marveled over them, staring in disbelief. She said to another teacher who happened to be in the room, "But look at these. He *answered* them." She was very much impressed. Needless to say, I ranked a very high percentile in the Math section of that achievement test. By the way, in those days, 1974, you didn't fill in circles. You manually answered the questions. Computers didn't grade students' achievement tests until the next year, 1975.

3rd Grade

The next year was indeed a much better year for me, and I had a marvelous teacher named Rayola Bagwell, a 31-year-old single teacher who knew how to communicate with her students. My parents knew about her, and they were very pleased that I had been placed in her classroom. As far as social development is concerned, I really soared that year. I felt so much more welcome in that classroom than the previous year that I got rid of my wrong voice. I felt more relaxed. I made some more friends, and I talked normally with my classmates. Several friends came out to my house to play, and I went to their houses, also. I did very well in Reading and Math, and my social development normalized to the point that the psychological assessment team terminated their monitoring and recognized that I belonged in the classroom just like everyone else.

Miss Bagwell taught us a very important topic called *Communication*. I have a picture of her at her desk, and beside the desk was a bulletin board with communication topics pasted on it. She took us on various field trips, one to see the telephone exchange, which at that time was on crossbar and would remain so for another 10 years until 1985. That was quite a place with all the electro-mechanical switches and relays. We also went to WSM and toured the TV studio where we were on Teddy Bart's Noon Show.

Miss Bagwell was an extraordinary woman and was one of my favorite teachers throughout my whole school career. I am grateful to her for helping to bring me out of my world and more into everyone else's.

How I Think and Remember

This is as good a place as any to explain to the reader how I think and remember. I consider it unique, compared to most people and the way they think.

Some autistics, for example Temple Grandin, think in pictures. They have a visual memory or a photographic memory. I have a good memory for numbers, events, and long ago conversations, but my memory is not photographic. Granted, I see plenty of images in my mind while I'm dreaming, and I dream in color, but while I'm awake, I cannot see visual images in my mind, not even while my eyes are closed. Still, for example, I have the ability to recognize a person's face, and in my mind, I know what he or she would look like, but it's a memory, not a visual image. I can remember quite a lot of shapes and designs, for example types of trees, cars, and telephone styles, but I cannot see those images in my mind.

As an analogy, my memory could best be described or compared to Microsoft DOS® on a computer, while those with photographic memories would be compared to Microsoft Windows®. I can't even see images of text in my mind, but somehow I'm a good speller, and I know in my mind how a word should look, with correct spelling and lettering.

I don't even see phone numbers in my mind, but I have quite a lot of them (hundreds) memorized. I remember the phone numbers of many friends and relatives, even including the phone numbers of a few friends I had back in Kindergarten and 1st grade.

My memory for events and how they happened is pretty accurate, and as far as I know, my memory doesn't change over time. People tell me I have a good memory. For various reasons, a lot of people's memories change, and some get repressed or even forgotten. Emotional reasons could have something to do with that. For me, I remember almost everything regardless of emotional factors.

Feelings, Psychiatric Assessment

Even though I did make vast improvements in the social areas, and even though the psychological assessment team recognized that I belonged in the normal classroom, I still had some social problems due to being an Asperger's. My parents were concerned for me, and they sought the help of a psychiatrist in Nashville named Dr. Henry Coppolillo. A Dr. Susan Lewis administered a psychiatric assessment test of a bunch of questions that I answered very well, except for feelings, which I didn't understand too well. Granted I had feelings, but I didn't know what to say in terms of talking about them. They were so complex for me at the time. The truth is, not all 10 year olds can be expected to understand feelings very well. That comes later on with maturity and becoming an adult.

In the same day, I had a meeting with the psychiatrist, Dr. Coppolillo, who came across to me as a nice man who showed compassion and concern. I could relate to him, and I liked him well enough to invite him to come visit us on the farm and see my woods. He was honored by my invitation and realized that I trusted him.

While I was never formally diagnosed with autism or Asperger's Syndrome, I was indeed diagnosed with psychological problems that, according to Dr. Lewis, needed serious attention *right away*. My diagnosis was labeled "adjustment reaction to childhood" and later "adjustment reaction to adolescence." That was in 1976 when I was in 4th grade. My psychological state was labeled in accordance with the terminology available during that time, the mid 1970's.

See, it wasn't until December 1993 that The New Yorker magazine printed Oliver Sacks' article, "*An Anthropologist on Mars*," which was an in-depth story and interview about the struggles and accomplishments of a famous high functioning autistic named Temple Grandin. The next year, Oliver Sacks published his book with the same title, all of which caused the works and discoveries in the 1940's of Hans Asperger of Austria and his medical description of autism to come more into the forefront, after having been confined for nearly 50 years in that country. It wasn't until 1991 that Hans Asperger's descriptions were translated to English. Finally in 1994, Asperger's Syndrome was included and officially listed by the American Psychiatric Association in the *Diagnostic and Statistical Manual of Mental Disorders, Fourth Edition (DSM-IV)*. This broadened the viewpoint of autism and also broadened the scope of diagnosis. While a Leo Kanner of Baltimore, Maryland had also researched the topic and had medically described autism at the same time as Hans Asperger, the concept was not so fully understood until Asperger's works were translated and made public. If the terminology had been in existence in the 1970's when I was a child, I would have been diagnosed as being a high functioning autistic, that is, Asperger's Syndrome.

A week later when the test results were ready, I met again with Dr. Coppolillo. I remember he commented that I did very well on the test that Dr. Lewis had administered, but the feelings section was deficient and needed some attention right away. I had an above average vocabulary, and my only weak verbal area was in social comprehension and my ability to plan and interpret social situations. I felt better and more at peace in the woods and up in a tall tree than I did associating with certain people (those who I was incompatible with and those who humiliated me). I had told Dr. Lewis, "I don't work much with feelings," and "I don't think about feelings." Even though I had friends, they determined that my fears about the pain involved in relationships and also my feelings of inadequacy in social situations were what led me to isolate myself. Well, that was partly true, but some of it also had to do with living and growing up on a farm. No matter what, the fact remains that I did indeed have friends come out to play, and I also played and socialized with others at school.

I will admit that Dr. Lewis was indeed right about my fears of pain involved in relationships. I didn't want my feelings hurt nor did I want rejections. I had feelings, no doubt about that. It's just that they were personal and private, and

I didn't want to share my feelings with others.

They honed in on the feelings deficiencies, and Dr. Coppolillo and my parents decided that it would be best if I went to *weekly* consultations with a psychiatrist! While it was true that I was deficient in the feelings area, I thought the psychiatrist sector was overdoing it, that is, that they were making a mountain out of a molehill. Once a month would have been enough. Dr. Coppolillo was just leaving to go to Colorado, as it turned out, so they assigned me to a new psychiatrist from Lebanon (the country) named Dr. Kourany.

I resented weekly visits, and I was angry at my parents for that! Once a month, I reiterate, would have been enough. It was all the way in Nashville, 40 miles away. I wanted to be home playing up in the woods, riding my bicycle, or playing with my friends instead of occupying (losing) a whole afternoon after school with a non-productive and non-helpful psychiatric session. I didn't know what to tell the psychiatrist, and his favorite comment was, "What do *you* think?" We never talked about feelings, anyway. I used to talk to him about what I did at home, what I did in the woods, where I took bike rides, and who I played with. I can add that Dr. Kourany was a good man, calm mannered, and easy going, and I appreciate that he never pressured me nor coerced me.

There was one thing I didn't realize until recently, and that was that Dr. Lewis' test results and recommendation had stated: "This boy very quickly needs to be involved in an intensive treatment program, including psychotherapy and possibly a residential therapeutic milieu program." Milieu means environment or surroundings, and in that case would have meant a hospital environment surrounded by overwhelming treatment programs and therapists! For all I knew, that could have entailed electro-shock therapy, plus a round of shots and sedatives, not excluding Thorazine! (*chlorpromazine*). Treatments like that were commonly used back in the 1970's. Based on Dr. Lewis' test results, and without my ever knowing it, that is, behind my back, Dr. Coppolillo strongly suggested to my parents that I be placed in such a dramatic inquisition! That would have meant taking me out of school, separating me from my routine, and institutionalizing me for weeks or even months! Plus, it would have been an embarrassment for me when I would have explained to my peers and classmates why I disappeared for a while!

Since I am writing this book, my parents came forth and only recently informed me of these shocking details! They have assured me, well that is, they have told me that the shock therapy, shots and sedatives would *not* have been administered. That was not a common practice in Nashville, even though many other hospitals across the nation relied on those procedures. Besides, that type of therapy was not administered to children. It was more commonly used with adults. What they would have done is talk with me and get me (well, coerce me) to more openly express my feelings.

They told me that Dr. Coppolillo had recommended a residential therapy program because he was concerned about me because as I enter puberty, I would have more hormones flowing through me and would therefore go into rages as a result. With that can of worms opened, I am now thankful to my parents that they said NO to that type of treatment!

The truth is, I *never* became violent, and certainly not in my teenage years either. It never even crossed my mind to become that way. Why were those psychiatrists so concerned about me? Even though I was never placed under the treatment they recommended, I still never became violent, which proves that my parents made the correct decision, and that I never needed such dramatic therapy!

My parents, especially my father, were people who worried a lot, and while in one sense I can appreciate their concern, they were obsessed with it. Sometimes, being overly worried and obsessed with something can lead to serious complications and hinder a situation instead of help it. While they think the psychiatric sessions were helpful to me and that I was improving, the truth is that I improved because I was learning on my own through social interactions at school and playing with my friends.

Now, don't get me wrong. Psychiatrists have their purpose, and they are a great help to certain people with serious psychiatric problems. I admit there are some people with serious mental health problems and mental illnesses who need those types of doctors, but my mental health was not that much out of kilter to warrant that type of treatment, especially what Dr. Coppolillo suggested! As a 10-year-old child, I had my ways of thinking and interpreting life. In all honesty, I believe some of my better teachers in elementary school, and certain friends I played with, were much better psychiatrists for me than the official ones in Nashville.

I also add comment that instead of a "residential therapeutic milieu program," a much better treatment for me would have been to go to a summer camp and enjoy activities and social interactions with kids my age. Well, in the summer of 1975 when I was out of 3rd grade, my parents actually tried to place me in Camp Country Lad up near Livingston, but the camp owner realized my quirks, shied away, and made up an excuse by saying, "I think he's too young." We had visited the place and had I liked it. I was very disappointed when he turned me down!

The way he found out about my quirks comes from a classic example of small town gossip. One day, his wife was at the grocery store in Monterey, where she happened to see a friend of my parents. They got to talking about me, and that friend of ours leaned over to her and quietly informed her that I didn't talk in Kindergarten. *Oh, my lord!* She subsequently took the news home and warned her husband. That was it when he found out about that! He didn't want any problem children, as if I were going to be a problem. Really, I had greatly overcome many of my quirks since Kindergarten!

Two years later, I joined the Boy Scouts at age 12, and there I did make some friends. We did campouts every season, plus plenty of other activities. We hiked the Appalachian Trail for a week one summer. Plus there was summer camp for a week at Camp Boxwell. I earned merit badges and I achieved. I became an Eagle Scout by age 15, and I enjoyed the National Scout Jamboree the following summer at Fort A.P. Hill, Virginia. Boy Scouts was an enriching experience for me, and I will always be glad I joined it and stayed with it for my adolescent years.

I continued to visit Dr. Kourany right through my senior year in high school, but *not* once a week, mind you! After the first year, I convinced my parents to reduce those visits to once a month or even less. As I entered puberty and developed feelings for girls, I for the first time, talked to Dr. Kourany about feelings.

Seeking an Official "Asperger's Syndrome" Diagnosis?

While writing this book, my parents have worried that if I don't seek an official "Asperger's Syndrome" diagnosis, officials, including Ph.D.'s and clinicians, might challenge the validity of this book.

Though I was not diagnosed with the "Asperger's Syndrome" label, I must state that I was indeed diagnosed three different times during my childhood, with the terminology available to clinicians and psychological assessment teams in *those* days.

I remind the reader that the first time was in 1968 with Ann Sitton at the Bill Wilkerson Center in Nashville. I was diagnosed with "elected mutism."

The second time was in 1972 by the psychological assessment team of Dr. Murphy Thomas and Dr. Jack Schnelle, in Murfreesboro. I was initially diagnosed by them as having problems of adjustment. Plus I "displayed a variety of aberrant behavior patterns."

The third time was in 1976 by Dr. Susan Lewis and Dr. Henry Coppolillo, in

Nashville. My diagnosis was labeled "adjustment reaction to childhood" and later "adjustment reaction to adolescence."

In my case, for the childhood traits I had, if I were a child today with the same traits, I believe that I would be diagnosed with Asperger's Syndrome, considering *today's* terminology.

Clinicians who read this book are going to think what they like, but there is no need for me to seek an official diagnosis of "Asperger's Syndrome" now, when I was already diagnosed three times in childhood, according to 1970's terminology. Besides, I'm not a child anymore, and I truly think the diagnosis name "Asperger's Syndrome" should have been attached to my condition *then*, not now, a quarter century later. What's more, the whole theme of this book is about *overcoming* Asperger's Syndrome, and seeking a diagnosis for my condition now would contradict the whole basis of this book. Plus a diagnosis would place a *lock*, that is, lock in a viewpoint in most other people's minds on how they would see me . . . as an *impaired* person, which I'm not.

Now, going back and redefining the diagnosis of my childhood, with present-day terminology, is a definite possibility, because back then I did have the traits of what clinicians today call "Asperger's Syndrome." I have Xerox copies of some 50 pages of literature dealing with the diagnoses of my childhood, including copies of the letters and weekly progress reports done by the psychological assessment team when I was in 1st and 2nd grades. So, I have my evidence. It seems that any clinician would clearly see that based on the literature and test results done during my childhood, and reading my anecdotes throughout the adolescent section of this book, that I did have what is now called "Asperger's Syndrome." Based on the terminology in those days, and considering the tests that I underwent during childhood, I did indeed receive valid diagnoses.

And let's not forget that an official diagnosis now (for something I have for the most part overcome) could entail two to three days of intensive testing, and it could also be quite expensive. In other words, it is just not worth spending a sizeable chunk of money for a diagnosis that is no longer necessary.

Granted, simply redefining my childhood diagnosis would be a lot simpler and cheaper.

In any rate, the facts remain that I was diagnosed three times in childhood, that I did indeed have aberrant behavior patterns in early childhood, and the anecdotes I present in this book are indeed true.

4th Grade, Listening Problems

After having Miss Bagwell for 3rd grade, I entered 4th grade. My teacher was Mrs. Stratford, and she was tall at 5' 10½". She was a temperamental type and was *not* one of my best teachers. She thought I had listening problems. I remember her one day calling me up to the side of her desk where she quietly lectured me, telling me that if I don't improve my listening skills, I would be punished. She also rudely added with trembling anger in her voice, "Ohhh . . . sometimes I feel like shaking you!" That made me quite angry, and when I went home that afternoon, I told my parents what my teacher felt like doing to me! My parents got right to it and had a serious talk with her, resulting in another lecture from her, this time in private in the bookstore closet of the front office! I told her it would take me about a month for me to become perfect, and she then told me, "I don't *want* you to be perfect." Yes, she did! After all, Mrs. Stratford was a perfectionist, and if she hadn't wanted me to be perfect, she wouldn't have gone to all the fuss! The problem lay in the fact that she would give instructions, and I would get right on the assignment, and as I was working on it, she had a bad habit of adding, "Oh, by the way, do it this way, etc. . . ." I was already well into the assignment, concentrating on it, and tuning out everything else.

That same day that Mrs. Stratford made that uncalled-for comment about shaking me, I had just one hour earlier thoughtfully brought from home and given her a Chinese Air Plant seedling, and still she had the audacity to tell me how she would like to shake me! Well, the first opportunity I had, I took that plant off her desk and took it back to mine. She soon discovered it missing, and never realizing why I took it back, she accused me of "Indian giving." She asked me to give it back to her. I wouldn't do it. I hope it dawned on her later that I took it back to get the message across to her that I don't approve of being shaken, not even for teachers to contemplate it!

There was another morning when Mrs. Stratford was trying to teach us some grammar lessons, and we weren't understanding it well enough. She became extremely impatient and inexcusably frustrated with us, and she counted out loud to 10 to avoid blowing her top! Even still, she scared all of us, and as I look back on it, I should have walked out of the classroom, marched right to the principal's office, and requested they sent the woman home for the day! Of course, at age 10, that didn't occur to me. Plus, children are afraid to do that. Temperamental people with emotional problems should not be teachers.

Even though she never actually paddled anyone, she made threats such as,

"If you don't bla bla bla, I'm going to paddle you so hard, you won't be able to sit down for a week!" Now that is a horrible thing to say to anybody, especially to a child! Those teachers should have been taught in their university training *not* to say comments like that to their students, not to even think that!

Despite her not being the best teacher, Mrs. Stratford was nice to us at times. I did make some more friends, and several of them came out to play. There were some good moments that year in school. We did take some field trips, and we did a lot of activities pertinent to 1776 and the Bicentennial. One day, we went over to the nearby house of one of my classmates. His mother was good friends with the teacher. The whole day was colonial style, and we made crafts, cut things out of construction paper, and cooked food like they did it 200 years ago. I learned a lot about the Bicentennial and the colonial days of early America.

At the end of the year, we all had a day at my house on the farm. I enjoyed having all my classmates visit. We played around the house, swung on some ropes that I had hung from one of the trees. We played in the tree house, and went down to the barns and haylofts where we played some more. We also went up in the woods. That was a treat as far as I was concerned, and it was a great day for all of us.

To add a side note, my 4th grade teacher did do one thing the next year which somewhat made things right and compensated for her previous year's bad behavior. She came along at the right moment, and in the hall, she talked my 5th grade teacher, Mr. Harrell, out of paddling several of us, over a matter of throwing peanuts in the lunchroom. She suggested that he have his students write letters and take them home to their parents, a good suggestion. Though he had paddled students on a regular basis and was a person who never knew how to apologize, he miraculously took her suggestion. That was the closest I ever came to being paddled, and thanks to her I was spared, and I preserved my perfect record throughout my whole school career.

To explain to the reader why I wrote that Mr. Harrell was a man who never knew how to apologize, there was an incident one afternoon after school while I was in 4th grade. As I was walking down the hall to the parking lot to be picked up by my mother, a patrol boy was treating me very rudely and was being bossy. So, I told him off. Mr. Harrell happened to be walking down the hall and heard the ruckus. Instead of rightfully calling down the patrol boy, like he should have done, he immediately shouted at me, "Hey! Shut up! Get on!" That made me angry and hurt my feelings! In anguish and frustration, I ran out of the hall to the parking lot, got into mother's car, and began crying. I told her what had just happened.

Well, that night, my parents called Mrs. Boyd, the special education teacher, and they told her how upset I was. The next day, she came to Mrs. Stratford, and she took me out of class. We walked down the hall to Mr. Harrell's class, where he was pulled from his class. In the hall, we talked some 10 minutes about the incident, and I requested an apology. Well, he explained that I was the one who had been wrong, to have "smarted off" to that patrol boy, and he saw no need for an apology. Even though Mrs. Boyd was mediating, and even though I reiterated that the patrol boy had been rude and bossy, Mr. Harrell would not apologize. So, we finished the talk, and Mrs. Boyd returned me to Mrs. Stratford's class.

No matter what, Mr. Harrell should have had enough compassion to try and make me feel better, that is, to *apologize* to me. Plus, they should have brought that patrol boy to me to apologize, as well. Instead, I was left feeling frustrated and very dissatisfied!

In general, for those who *apologize*, it is much *easier* for me to forgive them.

While Mr. Harrel was my 5th grade teacher the next year, things for the most part went well. Even though he never apologized, I think he learned something that day because he was never that harsh to me again. We learned Tennessee History under him, and I was one of the few students who got a Plus (same as an A) in that subject.

I finish this topic with an important note to teachers and teachers in training. If I were a teacher, I wouldn't want to be remembered by my students, a quarter century later, as a person who didn't know how to apologize. I wouldn't want that kind of reputation in my students' minds. Teachers need to realize that some of their students are very sensitive. They need to humble themselves enough to apologize to their students when they're rude to them. After all, students have feelings, and they count too.

6th Grade

My last year at Bellwood Elementary School was 6th grade. I had Miss Charlene Norris, an extraordinary woman and good teacher. She cared about her students, was fair, and diligently prepared us for 7th grade. At Bellwood, we had never been on the letter grading system. Letter grading was the standard for grades 7 through 12. So, with that in mind, and with her willingness to prepare us better, she had her own letter grading system that went alongside Bellwood's plus/check/dot system. I then learned what letter grades meant, and

I am grateful that she prepared us ahead of time.

MTSU Campus School, the elite school, always took *their* 6th graders on a trip to Huntsville, Alabama to see the rocket and space center. None of the five city schools ever made the Huntsville trip. Well, Miss Norris decided to change that, and she got the other three 6th grade teachers together and talked the principal into approving the trip. I remember her returning to our classroom half an hour later. She had a smile of triumph on her face, and she declared, "We got it!"

A few weeks later, we all took a Trailways bus down there. What an interesting trip it was! I saw the actual first Space Shuttle craft, and that was in the days before it ever lifted off. We saw plenty of other sights and some big rockets, as well.

In April of that year, we took a wonderful trip to Land Between the Lakes in Kentucky and stayed a whole week. All 6th graders went there as part of Bellwood School's curriculum. We took hikes and saw many different sights each day. That was a great week, and I enjoyed the trail hikes. Since we stayed in cabins near the lakeshore, I collected 100 Crinoid Stem fossils from the lakeside.

All in all, I learned a lot in 6th grade. We studied various and different subjects. Also I became better accepted by my classmates and made more friends. What's more? They appreciated me for my intelligence.

At the end of the year, Miss Norris took all of us out to my house, and we enjoyed the day on the farm, much like two years earlier at the end of 4th grade.

Before I move on to the next topic, I want to express my appreciation to two more teachers at Bellwood: Mrs. Porter and Mrs. Malone, for encouraging me to be a writer and for their support. I had written some short stories in 5th grade, and Mrs. Porter kindly ran off some ditto copies of my manuscript to send to different publishers. Although my stories were never published, those two teachers' encouragement sparked my interest in becoming the writer that I am today.

7th Grade, Overwhelming Feelings

In 7th grade, I entered a new school called Central Middle School. I had some good teachers who cared for us and prepared us well for high school. There were lots more students at this new school, and I met plenty of classmates from the other city schools. I made some more friends. A few of them were those who I remembered from my 2½ months of 1st grade at Campus School.

For my two years in middle school, things went very well.

This was the year that I also entered puberty. My feelings developed, and some of the feelings were quite strong, such as crushes on several girls, for example. Sometimes the feelings were overwhelming and embarrassing, making it hard to concentrate on whatever I was doing and sometimes making it difficult to talk to that certain girl that I had special feelings for. This was a pertinent matter that I did indeed talk over with the psychiatrist, Dr. Kourany, since I was seeing him anyway. He had thankfully quit saying, "What do you think?" so much. While he was calm mannered and easy going, and though he had some comments for me about it, there was nothing novel or outstanding that he told me. My feelings persisted. I wanted to continue with just normal feelings, but those overwhelming crush feelings were quite bothersome and were just too much for me. I didn't want them. So, I squelched them. It was one of the hardest things I ever did. I have understood from 7th grade forward, what the phrase "Cupid's arrow flew" means. Now yes, I still have feelings for people even today, but the level is no longer intense and is much more normal and manageable.

During 7th grade, some of the teachers organized a trip to New York City, Philadelphia, Washington DC, and Williamsburg. It was a great trip that I signed up for right away, and it was the first time I travelled outside the supervision of my parents. We all boarded a Trailways bus (with a 4-speed standard shift) and pulled away from Central Middle School March 16, 1979. It was an all night trip, our first stop being Thomas Jefferson's home, Monticello, near Charlottesville, Virginia, followed by several days of seeing the sights at Washington DC. After that, we went on up to New York City and did many activities, including going up into the Statue of Liberty and up to the top of the World Trade Center, elev. 1377 feet. What views indeed! Then we went to Independence Hall in Philadelphia, followed by seeing Williamsburg, Virginia and then making an all night bus ride back to Murfreesboro, arriving March 25. It was a packed trip, and I enjoyed the trip very much.

In addition to enjoying the trip, there was something else I remember very well, something I wanted to accomplish but didn't know how and/or felt uncomfortable. One young girl who I really had a crush on was also along on that trip, and one night in New York City, there was a Broadway presentation called "Sweeny Todd" that we all went to. Well, the thing to do was to take a date, and all the guys on the trip were making their choices. One night we all went to a movie, and I attempted to ask her by talking to her, but I somehow didn't make it to the question of actually inviting her. The next night, I went to the hotel room to ask her, and when I asked others if I could speak to her, she came out into the hall and asked, "What?!" in an exasperated manner. The sharp pain that I felt was too much for me, and instead of asking her for the date, I replied that it was nothing. When the Broadway presentation took place the following night, I noticed that she went with another guy who also escorted three other dates, a total of four to that show! What a hog! I felt sad that I couldn't take her. I didn't want to take somebody else, so I took no one. The show was loud, so I put my earplugs in. As it turned out, I fell asleep shortly after the show began, and in short order, the 3-hour show was over. I had enjoyed the sleep and felt well rested!

So much for dates. I have to admit that the pain I feared in relationships was certainly brought to the forefront when the young girl responded to me with, "What?!" I just didn't want anything to do with dates after that, and I have done very little dating since. Of course I realize there are plenty of other girls I could have enjoyed some fine dates with, but I simply lost interest in that type of social activity. I had more interesting things to do, namely travelling and enjoying adventures. Now don't get me totally wrong. I have indeed had friendships with girl classmates through high school and college, but only with those who I felt comfortable around, no *special* feelings. There were even some girls who I really liked. It's just that I never made the commitment of "going with them" or taking them on dates.

High School and College Years

As I attended high school, I did very well and made nearly straight A's. I was second in the class of 320 students. My IQ was measured at 130. Most of the people liked me, and I fit in pretty well. I had plenty of friends. Several times, I enjoyed doing activities with them, playing in sports with some of them, and marching in the high school band one of those years. I ran track for two years, doing the mile and the 880. I was even rushed to join a fraternity, except I turned it down because they drank and had keg parties. In high school, I had more freedoms, especially pertaining to where I could eat my lunch, and I could visit with *anyone* in the lunchroom, not just those from my homeroom.

I need to mention that there were times, especially during my first year of high school, where I experienced exclusion from my friends. I remember several incidents during group activities, say when we gathered in the auditorium. I walked in with who I saw as my better friends, and as we took our seats, it turned out all too often that they did it in such a way that they perfectly occupied *all* of the seats in that row! There was no seat left for me. As a result, I had to go sit somewhere else, and I felt a little bit excluded.

I experienced less of that after my freshman year, and things improved. I made a good number of friends in high school. Some of them became great friends. We did things together, and they would come out to my house and camp up in the woods with me. I still know some of them today.

In my senior year, I was voted the Most Intellectual, an honor indeed. I also received several awards for being first in the class. One was the Spanish Award, and another was the Geometry Award, plus the Advanced Math Award. I even topped out the Valedictorian in those areas. Being second in my graduating class, I was the Salutatorian, and I had understood that not only does the Valedictorian speak at graduation, so does the Salutatorian.

Well, in the spring of my senior year, I received the surprising news that it was decided (new policy) that only the Valedictorians speak at graduation. How strange! As I look back on it, maybe I should have contested it, but I just didn't. I believe when they realized I was going to be the Salutatorian, they purposefully fabricated a new policy to prevent me from speaking. Very clever! Plus, I will mention that there were certain clubs that met every two weeks during alternate schedule. One was called the Key Club, and all of the better students were invited to be members. I had never been invited, and I noticed that I was excluded. I don't think it has to do so much with my having been an Asperger's as much as the probable fact that a few of the faculty, those who happened to be in charge of that decision, just didn't like me. I have seen them several times since then, by chance, and they are always cold shouldered to me. Now don't get me wrong. Most of my teachers genuinely liked me, and that even included the principal and some of his assistants.

Once I graduated, I was glad to be through with high school. Even though I enjoyed many things about it, the curriculum and work load were intense! Even still, I knew I would miss my friends.

The following autumn, I entered Tennessee Technological University, in Cookeville, and I stayed in the dorms. It was quite an adjustment, being roommates with a total stranger. Things didn't go too well for the first two weeks, and one night he had his girlfriend in bed with him and denied me access to my room! I objected, and boy did he get defensive! I moved out the next day, and I became quite angry when I suddenly discovered that he had urinated in my water canteen! Well, in his little refrigerator, he had a bottle of Gatorade, the perfect drink to mask the taste. You can imagine what I did. I really enjoyed doing it, and I never told him either!

I had just become friends with a fellow from Kentucky, and he let me move in. The rest of the year went great. I made plenty of friends, and we did activities together. Some of them even took me home with them during a weekend. Some of them came to my house and farm to visit. One of them even travelled with me to Cumberland Island in Georgia. I succeeded. I actually made a good number of friends, and though we've all drifted apart since then, I look several of them up from time to time. At the end of the first year, my roommate paid me a high compliment by saying, "God could not have created a more considerate, friendly roommate." He also told me that it was nice to not have to worry about what shape his room would be in each time he walked in.

Cookeville was a somewhat small town, and I used to take regular bike rides out of town. I kept a map on the wall and marked all the roads I explored by bicycle. The countryside was scenic, but it was hilly. There were times when friends of mine took bike rides with me.

The school curriculum of Electrical Engineering was tough, and I made plenty of B's and C's, to go along with many A's. Even through my last final exam, I felt like they were trying to weed us out! My QPA, when I graduated, was barely over a 3.0, out of a 4.0 maximum, which was still quite good for a EE. I had to study a lot, and at times, I felt mental blocks with the vague theories and abstract concepts. Calculus, Differential Equations and Complex Variables were not straighforward like the math I had previously studied in high school, and it was much harder for me to understand it. Of all the math courses I took, I made only one A (Calculus III).

Nevertheless, I enjoyed making friends, and even though I refused to join fraternities, I enjoyed the social side more than the curriculum. Several classmates used to study with me and do homework with me, especially the last year. When I graduated, I felt sad because I knew I would miss my friends.

Since that time, not being in school, it's not been as easy to make friends.

*　　*　　*

Robert Sanders typing to 10,000, July 1972

Robert Sanders with his dog "Puppy", January 1974

field trip in 3rd grade, April 1975

Robert Sanders looking at the globe, 1972

PART 2

PROJECTS & INTERESTS

Travelling

Since I was a child, I have liked to travel. When I became 16 and could drive, I began to travel on my own. When I was 18, I travelled up to Canada and visited some friends in Toronto. In the summer of 1985, between my first and second year of college, I drove my 1970 Ford Fairlane station wagon out West for 7 weeks. I took my bicycle and backpack and enjoyed the trip very much. I was 19, and I had to take the whole trip alone, which wasn't exactly my choice. I had sincerely searched, even advertised, for a travelling companion to take the trip with me, but I had no takers. I backpacked and camped in several parks and wilderness areas, and I climbed several mountains. I must admit that I felt lonely at times during my first trip out there, but I got used to it and have made several more trips out West and to other areas of this country, plus Canada and Mexico since then.

I had saved money through high school, and I took a year off from college to work and travel. I flew to Australia and New Zealand and was there for several months during their summer of 1985-1986. Again, I took my bicycle and backpack. In Australia, I did some wilderness backpacking, using topo maps and a compass. Australia is such a big country that I also bought a car and sold it back while I was there. It was convenient for the road trip I took and for sleeping in at nights. In New Zealand, I travelled much of the time on my bicycle, and I enjoyed the scenery there, as well. I made several friends in both countries, and I still know some of them today.

From 1986 forward, I took on a project of hiking sections of the Pacific Crest Trail each time I was out West. Though I didn't hike the whole trail all in one season like some do it, I have enjoyed numerous sections, and I have some great pictures of the excellent scenery in some areas. I also wrote detailed diary accounts of my trail hikes, which include descriptions of the terrain, scenery, plus the types of trees and wildflowers seen along the way. Sometimes I have met people while hiking, but I have only been able to keep up with very few through the years.

Before my final year of college, I took another year off to work and travel. I returned to Australia and New Zealand, and I took my bicycle and backpack with me again. The same as 4 years earlier, I bought a car and sold it back. It was nice to see and explore more of Australia and New Zealand, and I feel fortunate that I was able to do it. I also enjoyed looking up friends who I had known 4 years earlier, and I made some new friends, as well.

In more recent years, I have taken my bicycle and backpack over to England and Scotland where I have gone walking and camping on some of their trails and rights of way. The countryside is great for bicycling, and I have bicycled for days, even weeks, through the English countryside, camping each night in farmland or in woods.

Travelling has been one of my favorite things to do in life, and I have also enjoyed meeting and associating with people along the way.

The Bicycle Rides Project

At age 10, I began to bicycle on the local back roads in the county, and I enjoyed the rides through the farmland. Starting at age 11, I decided to begin a project of riding on *every* back road and highway in the southwest portion of the county. My strong desire to explore and my thoroughness had driven me to accomplish the task. On selected weekends, I chose certain roads and made various bicycle rides. In those days, the late 1970's, more than half of the roads were gravel. Since 1990, all but a very few of those roads have been paved.

I had a map of the county on my bedroom wall, and I used to mark with a red felt tip pen the roads on which I had bicycled.

I remember one favorite country store I used to visit called Versailles Grocery, run by a nice lady named Mrs. Carlton. She used to cook lunch for several locals each day. It was set in a beautiful hilly area of the county, and occasionally friends used to ride with me to that store.

One day, I rode to a community called Newtown, and I got caught in a downpour of rain. As a result, I had to call my parents to come and get me. Since I had to be picked up instead of riding home myself, those roads didn't count, and I had to bicycle there again on a better day to make that right.

By the time I was 13, I had completed my project, even reaching and covering all the back roads on the west side of Eagleville. So, I next advanced to cover all of the back roads to the east of the southwest portion, the entire southeast portion of the county. Now I would cover every back road within a 15 to 22 mile radius of my home, depending on the direction. I was 15½ when I made my final ride to complete the coverage of the furthest roads from me, some of them as much as 22 miles from my house at a community called Readyville. A couple of those bicycle rides had been 90 miles long! I also covered some of the roads in the northwest portion of the county, those that were nearest me.

In addition to that major project at age 15½, I decided to ride my bicycle to and from my grandparents' house in Crossville, 100 miles away. I succeeded, riding there in 8 hours 25 minutes, having left home at 5:52 AM and arriving at 2:17 PM. My grandparents were sitting in the front yard at the time, and my grandmother upon seeing me commented, "Well, I'll declare!" They were both impressed, and my grandfather complimented me by telling me I sure was smart to have been able to ride all that way. I rested there the second day and returned home on my bicycle the third day. It was quite a trip, and I remembered how several people had earlier told me it would not be possible, that my legs would just not handle such a long ride. I was glad to have proven them wrong on that one!

To add to the amazement, I did all of that bicycle riding on a regular one-speed bicycle. I finally bought a multi-speed bicycle at the age of 18.

Radio DXing

When I was age 9, I started listening to the radio. It is important to mention that while I like it quiet a lot of the time, there were also times that I listened to the radio, especially the AM band. I used to enjoy picking up stations from faraway cities, and I kept a detailed log book of all the stations I had received. In other words, I was a DXer, and the furthest station I ever received on AM was KSL from Salt Lake City, Utah. I never ever picked up any from California.

My favorite radio station was (in those days) Musicradio WLS 890 from Chicago, Illinois. They played mostly pop songs, and I liked a lot of those songs, especially from the 1970's and 1980's. I have a record collection from those days. Of course, I was forced to change over to CDs when vinyl records stopped being made on a grand scale around 1990.

I liked listening to two disk jockeys: John Landecker and Larry Lujack. John did a "WLS Boogie Check" every night around 9:30 PM when people would call in, and he occasionally did "Can I Get a Witness News," where he would ask famous people questions, and for their answers he would play excerpts of recordings of their speeches. It was hilarious! Larry Lujack did a funny "Show Biz Report" every morning around 7:30 AM.

I began DXing in 3rd grade, and I did more of it in 5th grade. My parents bought me a GE 10 band radio, which I still have in good condition. With that,

I added quite a bit to my log book. When summer came, I got away from it and then returned to DXing in 7th grade. Again, I entered into my log book a lot more first time receptions for more stations. I had quite a list. Since 7th grade, I have pretty much gotten away from DXing.

By the mid 1980's a lot of stations like WLS went off clear channel, and a lot more radio stations were added by permission of the FCC! I am disappointed by the overloading of the AM band. Back in 1979, when I first visited California, I actually picked up WLS out there, and also WWL from New Orleans, but that sort of phenomenon is no longer possible.

One can see the traits of a high functioning Asperger's, considering all the detailed records of DXing that I used to keep. In a way, my listening to the radio was a portrayal of my desire to communicate.

There was one really positive benefit that came from my radio DXing. When I was in 5th grade, I wrote letters to some 50 radio stations across the country, asking them how they got their call letters and what was the furthest place they had received a reception letter from? Most of them replied. WLIJ, a 1,000 watt station from nearby Shelbyville, Tennessee, actually sent me a copy of their furthest reception letter, a long and detailed letter from Toronto, Ontario. I wrote the fellow, and we became DXing pen pals, and later just pen pals when the DXing interests went by the wayside. He and his family are the friends I went to visit after high school, when I was 18. Some of his cousins were also visiting, and we went hiking in one of the provincial parks. I still know him and his family to this day, and they are nice people.

The March 1 Sleet Storm

I was in 8th grade, and on Saturday, March 1, 1980, a sleet storm arrived! I had made plans for a good friend of mine named Chris to come out to the farm and visit for the whole day, and of course the sudden weather change for the worse caused the plans to be cancelled.

Chris and I were going to go hiking up in the Versailles Hills a few miles southwest of the farm. I was willing to go anyway, but the roads were so bad and icy that Chris' father said he wouldn't be able to bring him. Plus, it was too cold! Needless to say, I was disappointed.

Chris couldn't come, and I couldn't make that happen. (He finally came out April 5, as it turned out.) I had to accept that change in that day's plans, but there was one thing that I refused to let be changed . . . that walk. Despite a strong north wind, falling sleet and snow, and 20° F temperature, I put on my snowsuit, wool hat, and boots, and I walked over there and climbed that hill regardless! I made it just fine to the top, and it looked very different up there with sleet covering the ground. I walked back home without mishap, and the hike went well. A unique day it was indeed.

Schools were closed on Monday, March 3, by the way, the only time schools were ever closed any day in March for snow and ice. Of course, there was the blizzard in mid March 1993, but that was long after I was in school.

One can see that I was fixated on taking that hike, with or without Chris, and I also did it as a protest against the change in plans for the bad weather. So, the day was not a total loss, because I stubbornly made that part of the day right.

The Log Cabin Project

Ever since I was age 10, I had wanted to build a log cabin in the 90 acre woods on our farm. I was spending time in the woods on many afternoons, and I used to run around up there with my dog "Puppy" who I had found at my grandparents' house in 2nd grade. My dog and I used to run around a lot together when I was growing up, and I had her for 15 years. On occasion, we even camped up in the woods.

While I thought about the cabin and studied ways to build it, I cleared several trails in the woods. One day when scouting out a place for my cabin I came upon a rise that looked perfect for it. Two years later when I was 12, I had a few Hickory tree saplings removed that were growing exactly where I would build it. (I was still too young to use the chainsaw myself.) I left all the other trees in place, and they are great shade trees.

Finally, during my second year in high school, I decided to begin my project. My parents said I wouldn't be capable of doing it, but I proved them wrong on that one, and I began to build the cabin. I cut 77 Cedar logs, some 12 feet long, and others 17 feet, and I dragged each log up the trail to the site using ropes and roller logs. Using a chain saw, I notched the logs, and I assembled them. My father came up the trail to see my progress, and he was pleasantly surprised at how quickly the cabin was taking shape. I even put a loft in the cabin, and I completed it with a tin roof. I was very pleased with the finished product, a log cabin for me to enjoy. It was, in a sense, a nice get-away place that was secluded in the woods, and I'm glad that I built it.

Later that year, friends of mine came to visit, and other friends of my parents and relatives visited and saw the cabin also. Many of them were impressed. Several times, high school friends would come out on a Saturday, and we would sleep in the cabin. Even a few friends from college came and slept a night up there with me.

I even installed phone service to the cabin, running army phone wire underground and along the forest floor to reach the cabin nearly half a mile from the main house. My parents had 2 army crank phones, and my friends and I would call home with them. Plus, we still had the first original telephone to the farmhouse, a wooden wall crank phone. I bought some 1.5 volt dry cell batteries and connected that telephone to the system also. That is actually when my interest in telephones began, and one can see that in a sense, I was displaying a desire to communicate.

The cabin still stands today, over 20 years later, and I still go up there and enjoy it at times. My trails are also still in place, and I maintain them every year.

The Typewriter Incident

In my senior year of high school, I was taking Typing so I could learn to type with all fingers instead of just hunt and peck. My parents had two typewriters at home, and both of them were manual typewriters. The high school had a modern fleet of IBM electric typewriters, all of them with the rapid rotating ball instead of proper keys, and they all had a return button instead of the lever.

I was somewhat disappointed that *all* of the typewriters were electric. The keys were so super sensitive. You even so much as *thought* about touching a key, and that ball would suddenly slam a letter on the piece of paper. At home at nights, I would practice the same typing lessons on the manual typewriter so I would be sure and know how to type properly on them, as well.

Well, one Sunday night, a few weeks into the Typing course, I was watching the *Disney Sunday Movie*. There happened to be a scene of a high school Typing class, and every one of the typewriters were Royal manual typewriters with normal return levers. It made me envious and made me wish the high school I attended would also offer the use of manual typewriters. Not a single one of the typewriters was manual.

So, I decided to fix that situation, at least for me, that is. My Typing class was 6th period, and right after 5th period, I walked to my car, and I with some difficulty carried my parents' heavy Royal manual typewriter to that class . . . managed to get it in there without the teacher noticing. I set the IBM typewriter on the floor beside me, placed the Royal manual typewriter in its place, and I started typing like everyone else.

Around 20 minutes into the class, the teacher noticed and commented with quite a bit of interest, "Well, what have we here? Where did *that* come from?" She had a smile on her face.

I couldn't help but laugh, and I explained to her that I brought it because I wanted to use a manual typewriter at least one day in class.

Many of my classmates remembered the unique typewriter incident for years to come.

Keeping Detailed Records

There are many ways through my life that I have kept detailed records, for one, the radio DXing. I already mentioned how I kept detailed daily accounts of my trail hikes. That not only includes my hikes along the Pacific Crest Trail, but also includes other major hiking that I have done, such as: the Alpine Walking Track in the mountains of southeast Australia, the Cradle Mountain-Lake St. Clair walk in Tasmania, and also the Pennine Way walk in northern England.

During my travels I have taken lots of great pictures of nature scenery, and I have my trip pictures in photo albums. Some of my best pictures are enlarged, and I have them hanging on the walls inside my house. In my earlier travels, I was using a Voigtländer camera, but now I mostly use an Olympus OM-1. Both of them take clear sharp pictures

When I first started backpacking, I didn't have any supply list to refer to, and I almost always forgot something on a hike. Well, in the summer of 1986, I remembered everything, and when I finished that hike, I decided to inventory *every* item in the backpack, including the food I took with me. That list became very useful to me in the future and saved me time in having to remember every detail.

When I was a child and teenager, I kept a written log of my dreams for several years. Then I got away from it. Ten years ago, I began writing down my dreams again, and I have been keeping a log of them ever since. Having a written record of my dreams helps me analyze life better. Plus, dreams are useful for ideas that I include in my novels.

Later on is a topic called *The Family Photo Albums Project* where you'll realize how I have kept detailed genealogical records. Not only that, I also keep a complete list of the addresses and phone numbers of my friends and relatives, with backup copies of all that data in another building, so that it *won't* get lost. To me, having friends and relatives is important.

Pertaining to friendships, I have written detailed overviews about my friendships with some of my better friends. Part of the reason I did that was to help me gain a better understanding of friendships and how they work. However, since 1997, I have gotten away from that because it was too time consuming to continue that precedent. Besides, I got busier with writing more novels, and my writing time was occupied by that.

Starting in 1983, when I bought my first car, my 1970 Ford Fairlane station wagon, I became more aware of station wagons with a 3-speed on the column. I only rarely saw one on the road. So, I started keeping a list on which I recorded each sighting, including the type of car and approximate year made. Some types of station wagons really surprised me, that they had a 3-speed on the column, and some of the more surprising ones were a 1974 Ford Country Sedan station wagon, and a mid 1970's AMC Matador station wagon. By the early 1990's, I had a list of some 30 sightings. 3-speed station wagons were pretty rare in the United States, but in Australia and New Zealand, they were pretty common.

While in Australia and also Great Britain, I took pictures of all the types of cars commonly seen on the road, took more than 100 pictures, and I compiled photo albums of those cars. Some friends who have looked at my albums were intrigued at how meticulous and thorough I was in compiling them.

Also when I was in Australia, I kept a detailed log book of my expenses, so I would know exactly how much a long trip like that cost me. Though I rarely consult the log book, it's nice to have the record in case anyone ever asks me how much a trip like that costs. I keep up with my business expenses the same way, and I have a thorough record when I report my income each year for tax purposes.

Pertaining to school, I kept all my homework and written assignments. I even made Xerox copies (for myself only) of all the music we played while I was in the band, both in middle school and high school. Two footlockers in the attic contain all the homework I did, one for high school and one for university. I collected all my textbooks, as well. I didn't sell them back, like a lot of students did.

In high school, it was a tradition for classmates to get yearbook signatures from each other. I made a point to get signatures and notes from all my friends and everyone I knew. Well, when I got to college, I was told that it was not the norm to collect yearbook signatures. "People don't do that in college," I was told by many. Well, I explained that I wanted to remember who my friends were, and I collected lots of signatures and notes. All but one person accommodated my request. It's nice to look back at those yearbooks and reminisce about my friends then. You know, I was the *only* one who ignored the norm and made a point to get yearbook signatures from all my friends.

Also, during my first year of college, there was almost no one there who went to high school with me. To help me learn the names of all my new friends, I kept a detailed list of names of everyone I met, including when and where for each one.

In a book called *Diagnosing Jefferson*, written by Norm Ledgin, I realized how Thomas Jefferson had many traits of being an Asperger's. He kept exact and thorough records of his spending, right down to the penny. He liked sameness, that is, he resisted change. He was also obsessed with finishing all of the details of his house, Monticello, among other traits. In many ways, Jefferson was a genius.

There are other ways that I also keep detailed records, as the reader will realize while reading the topics of this book.

The Ford LTD Station Wagon Project

For several years, while I was still in school, I had an obsession to take a later model full-size station wagon, a Ford LTD Crown Victoria, and put a manual transmission in it. It had annoyed me for quite some time that nearly all of America's mid-size cars, and all full-size cars since 1971, were mandatory automatic, except for pickup trucks, vans, and some suburbans. One couldn't even special order a big station wagon with a standard shift.

Well, when I got out of school, I made that situation right, at least for my uses, when I bought a 1980 Ford LTD Crown Victoria station wagon and installed an in-line 6-cylinder 240 motor and a 4-speed manual transmission out of a pickup truck. It became quite involved, as I found out, especially pertaining to installing the clutch and brake pedal assembly and having to fabricate the clutch linkage, fabricate motor mounts, and take careful precise measurements. Welding had to be done, but the project was a success, and I have driven that car on long trips, totaling more than 100,000 miles.

That was a major project that required tenacity and patience, and it was another triumph that showed how I begin a project and see it through to completion. One can observe that in one sense, I was obsessed with having a standard shift in a car that never carried that option. The fact that I got that 6-cylinder motor to fit in there was another triumph in itself. No Ford LTD Crown Victoria ever had an in-line 6, nor a standard shift.

My first car, which I still have, is a 1970 Ford Fairlane station wagon, with factory standard shift. While keeping it and still using it at times, I accepted enough change to get a newer car for long trips, but I don't like automatics. I didn't even drive the LTD Crown Victoria until I had converted it. A friend of mine drove the LTD Crown Victoria for me when I bought it, and he was the one who parked it on the concrete pad where I began the converting process.

After I finished the project, I compiled all of my receipts, and I wrote out a detailed list of my expenses, so I would know exactly what the project cost me. Plus, I wrote a complete account of all the procedures that were done to convert the car to standard shift.

It's a good feeling to know that I have a unique car, with a simpler engine and normal carburetor, not fuel injection, and no computer. My car is easier to work on, for which I feel better on long trips.

Collecting Things

Many people like to collect things, from coins to teaspoons to rocks and fossils. I like to collect most of those things too, and I even used to collect my own hair for several years after each haircut. I still like to collect things to this day, and rocks and fossils are some of those. However, there are some unique things I collect. Among them are old telephones, newspaper comics, and even trees and tree seeds.

From the time I was 8, I became interested in fossils, and I used to collect black fossilized shark's teeth from the beach in South Carolina. My family used to take me to Pawley's Island for a week every summer, and in addition to swimming in the ocean and walking and running up and down the beach, I spent part of each day hunting for shark's teeth in broken up shell deposits. I became very good at it, and I found and collected other types of fossils also. I used to keep count of how many teeth I found each day, and each year. Some years I didn't find so many, and other years, I found more than 1,000. It all depended if the previous year's weather had been calm or rough. The rougher it was, the more shark's teeth that got washed up for people like me to find them. Ranging from the years 1974 through 1992, I have found over 5,000 shark's teeth, and they are labeled in ex-medicine bottles with the year and how many there are.

I also got started hunting for and collecting fossils out of the creek bed on our farm in Tennessee. There weren't any shark's teeth there, but there were other types of fossils, including Crinoid Stems (locally called Indian money).

I remember back in 6th grade when my classmates and I were at Land Between the Lakes in Kentucky. Since the cabins were very near the lakeshore,

I discovered plenty of Crinoid Stems. So, I began to collect them. I realized I could find as many as 100, and I made it a project to achieve that number before we would return to Murfreesboro. Well, the final morning came up, and I had found 93 of them. I just had to find 7 more. So, despite the rules that we were not supposed to be down there by the shore early in the morning, I went on down there long enough to find and collect 7 more, to meet my requirement. I picked up number 100 right when one of the teachers caught me and informed me that I had broken a rule. It was Mr. Harrell, my former 5th grade teacher, and I made sure I did *not* apologize to him. However, they didn't punish me, since it was time to go back to Murfreesboro, and also since my father was there with us all week. My father understood my obsession about finding 100 Crinoid Stems, which he explained to the teacher, who then saw reason.

When I was age 9, I began collecting the Sunday edition of Dagwood comic strips, (*Blondie*). That was my favorite comic strip and still is. I always make a point to read it first. Anyway, I collected every Sunday's edition for 15 years. At the end of each year, I would staple the 52 pages together, but it was too thick for conventional staplers. So, I what I did was carefully puncture the left margins with an ice pick and I bound them with wire. In the autumn of 1986, The *Nashville Tennessean*'s comic styling suddenly changed, and Dagwood was no longer on the front page, which disappointed me! By the later 1980's, it was becoming too much trouble to continue collecting it. I was away at university by then and was also travelling at times. So, I decided to finally let it go. The end of 1989 was a good stopping point. No matter what, it's nice to have collected 1½ decades of Dagwood (*Blondie*).

I also like to collect old expired license plates that I find in car salvage yards. Some yards give them to me and others sell them. Plus, there are friends and relatives who have given me their old license plates. I have almost all 50 states collected.

As I began travelling on my own at age 17, I began to collect rocks from each place of interest that I visited, be it a beach, historic site, wilderness area trail, or a mountaintop. I now have a good collection of rocks from faraway places. Some of my rocks are in boxes in storage, and my better ones are displayed on shelving at home.

Collecting Old Telephones

In addition to rocks and fossils, I also like to collect old telephone instruments, and I have gathered quite a collection of dial phones, along with a few crank phones. Many of my phones are from other countries, and I have many countries represented. While travelling in other countries, I have visited the phone companies and telephone exchanges where I have requested old dial phones, for future use in a museum, and most of them have been friendly and accommodating. I appreciate old telephones in a time of such modern technology, and I still use dial phones to make calls and talk over. (I do have a touch-tone phone by its side to answer all those annoying "menu" selections.) It's my intention to create a telephone museum in the future.

To demonstrate one example of uniqueness in my collecting old telephones, when I was in New Zealand in 1986, I noticed that a lot of the small towns at that time (not anymore) had manual exchanges with operators to connect all calls. To be specific, Kaikoura with 3,000 people had a manual exchange with 9 operators. The telephones were made of black bakelite, and each one had a crank handle. Early the next year, I wrote the New Zealand Post Office (their phone company) and requested the possibility of selling me some of those crank phones. The postmaster wrote me back and said that Kaikoura had converted to automatic on October 15, 1986, and they were selling the old instruments for NZ $2 each. I wrote back and sent cash to purchase 3 of them, which including postage added up to around US $60. Upon receiving my money, he sent them in the mail to me by surface mail.

Several years later, I was travelling over in New Zealand again, and when going through Kaikoura, I talked to the Post Office. The postmaster was still there, and I thanked him for accommodating me by selling me and sending me those crank phones and that they were well appreciated. He surprised me by telling me that I was the *only* American who had corresponded with him and ordered crank phones.

The only one?! I had a moment of realization about how unique I am, well, how unique a lot of people are in this world. I just assumed that there would have been at least 10 or 20 Americans, including phone collectors, who would certainly have ordered crank phones from Kaikoura. Of course, there were plenty of other towns in New Zealand on manual exchange in those days, and some of them might have gotten the odd order from an American. However, as I think about it, I am likely the *only* American who got any crank phones from New Zealand at all.

By 1990 New Zealand was selling a lot of old dial telephones as well, some of them the GEC 332, the bakelite English style desk and wall phones. Touch-tone service was the latest rave, and towns were converting over as fast as possible. I purchased and surfaced mailed home several great telephones, which are greatly appreciated in my collection. What New Zealand was tossing, I was treasuring.

Telephone collecting has been a great hobby, and I like to compare the styles between different countries. Plus, telephones represent communication, which is something I always believe in doing. I also keep a complete inventory list of each type of telephone I have.

Not only have I collected telephones, I have also collected part of a step office (step by step telephone exchange). That was in 1995, when several small towns in Georgia were converting to digital. I tried to purchase the equipment from their local phone company, but the bureaucracy and red tape was so thick, that it wasn't allowed. So, I went around their system and talked to one of the tear out crews who kindly accommodated my wishes and sold me enough of each type of Strowger switch (20 of each) plus the other equipment necessary to make the exchange work. They "hired me as one of their employees" which permitted me to enter the exchange and help them tear it out. That was brilliant. I was 2 days with them cutting wires and carefully removing the Strowger switches, racks, and other equipment, which I placed inside a U-Haul trailer I had rented for the job. I was glad to be able to obtain that equipment, which I plan to install in the future phone museum that I want to build.

Collecting Trees

I also like to dig up tree seedlings and collect seeds. Ever since I was a young child, I have been interested in the trees of this world. Since age 8, I have known what tree is what, even with the leaves off in winter.

Trees are miracles that represent life. There are thousands of varieties of trees. They grow in many different types of environment here on planet Earth, and they cover much of the land surface. They give life by providing oxygen to all animals and humans as well, in addition to purifying the air and maintaining ground water stability. They also provide shade from the Sun. Many of them provide us food through their nuts, as well as providing us extracts for medicinal purposes.

Trees parallel the life cycles of humans in that they are born, grow to maturity, give their fruits, and eventually die. To humans, they give companionship the way they grow throughout the forests and gardens. Trees are not conditional like so many humans are. Trees are also not like humans in that they don't fight, they don't abuse, they don't threaten, they don't reject, they don't attack, and they are not aggressive. With the trees, one doesn't have to worry about complex family dynamics and problems.

To be a tree in the forest, such a *peaceful* existence.

While not removing any plant life from national park lands, I have dug up trees from roadsides and from national forests, and I have mailed them home. I sent home many varieties, and some of them lived. To this day, I have numerous Western Red Cedars from Washington. They do very well in Tennessee. I have a Douglas Fir, also from Washington, and I have an Incense Cedar from southwest Oregon. It's the fastest growing conifer I have. I also have a Ponderosa Pine from Idaho.

Trees that only lived a few years have been the Western Hemlock, Western White Pine, Giant Sequoia, and the Larch, or that is, Tamarack. I regret that one tree I have tried was never very successful, and that is the Giant Sequoia. They don't like Tennessee climate nor the soil, and the Coastal Redwoods have to be kept in pots so they can be brought in during winter.

From lands closer to home, I have a Balsam Fir from northern Minnesota. It is now 12 feet tall. I've had it for 18 years, since I brought it home as a tiny seedling in a fishing tackle box from a Boy Scout canoeing trip in 1984. It has done very well. Believe it or not, Fraser Firs from east Tennessee and North Carolina will *not* live here in middle Tennessee, but the Balsam Fir will.

Also in 1984, I collected from the slopes of Mt. Mitchell in North Carolina, a native American Chestnut tree seedling . . . was very surprised to find one. You see a lot of growths from stumps, but very few seedlings. It lived, and it's now over 20 feet tall! It has a trunk around 6 inches in diameter, and it's been blooming for the past 3 years, only the seeds have never been fertile. I have more recently brought home a second native American Chestnut tree as a pollinator. I hope they will continue to grow, and maybe one day I'll get some seedlings from them.

I have even collected trees and seeds from as far away as Australia and Tasmania. I grew some Black Cypress-Pines from Victoria, which I have given away to people in California, Mexico, and Florida, since they can't grow outside in winter. I have sent home seeds from various places and have grown many types of trees. Some did very well while others got barely started and died. While in Tasmania, I went to various nurseries and bought a King William Pine seedling and a Celery Top Pine seedling, and I successfully sent them home to

Tennessee. I declared the contents as a doll, gift, and it passed U.S. Customs without being caught. The King William Pine died within weeks, and the Celery Top Pine grew slowly for 7 or 8 months before also giving up.

No matter what, it has been one of my favorite past times to collect and care for trees, and I'm grateful that I live on a farm to have the space to plant them.

*   *   *

Robert Sanders and Lewis Collins taking a bike ride, September 1979

Robert Sanders and Jody Ruffner playing in the creek, April 1977

Robert Sanders and his igloo, January 1979

PART 3

FRIENDSHIPS

This next section of several topics deals with a very important issue, especially for autistics and Asperger's: the art of making and keeping friends. This section relates numerous stories and phenomena of my life, including success stories but also trials and tribulations. Also included are ideas, insights, reasons, and speculation. It is my hope that the reader will benefit and compare notes, which may lead to finding solutions for his/her own friendship situations.

Ideals of Friendship

We live in a day and age where most friendships are far from ideal. There are people who are hostile, and there are some people who hold grudges. Peace does not exist in every part of the world, nor does it exist in every family.

I suppose that a lot of people often have a longing desire for peace and friendship, the ideal kind, what most would call a utopia. While there are some people who have achieved that in this world, that is not the case for the large majority of the human population. Instead, many of us are aggressive and violent. Even nations are violent and at war with one another!

This is atrocious, considering that we are human beings, highly advanced mammals who have reasoning faculties and intelligence well above most mammalian species. Therefore, humans ought to know how to really be at peace with one another.

I have sometimes pondered on what it would be like to have an ideal friendship? With an ideal friend, you can feel 100% at peace and you can feel 100% comfortable in his/her presence. The ideal friend makes you feel good and feel rejuvenated when you're around him/her. An ideal friend is 100% honest and straightforward, invites you to join him/her on activities and enjoys your company. An ideal friend includes you and welcomes you into his/her home. An ideal friend lets you get close, is comforting and reassuring to you, is supportive, and cares for you and your well being. He/she is faithful, appreciates you, and is proud of you and your accomplishments. Most of all, an ideal friend is glad to have your friendship.

With an ideal friend, there is no such thing as shrieking or struggling away with abhorrence. There is no such thing as lying, avoidance, embarrassment, hostility, aggressiveness, fear, violence, and other negative traits.

Instead, there is 100% peace, love, trust, and honest friendship.

At times through my life, I have had dreams of being with one or more really good friends. Even though we don't know each other in real life, we do in the dream. We have visited with each other, enjoyed each other's company, and have gone places together. With some of those people I have dreamed about, the sense of peace and closeness of friendship I have felt is incredible. Sometimes I even remember their names after I wake up, and I feel like those friends are so real that surely I must know them in real life, but I don't. I wake up truly missing friends like that, and I wish I really knew them.

Good dreams like that instill a longing desire in me to search for ideal friends and find that type of peace.

Many people who are autistic and/or have Asperger's Syndrome have more difficulty in making really good friendships, even though their intentions are usually very good. They have quirks about them and idiosyncrasies, and they don't always know what to expect in social situations. As a result, many autistics have more of a yearning desire for real friends than most other people.

For an ideal society to exist, that is, a utopia, if you see someone who looks attractive or friendly, you ought to be able to walk right up to the person, introduce yourself, and become friends, just like that. Instead, we as a society have pigeonholed ourselves to various and sundry social rules and social cues that inhibit our free ability to make friends. Think about it. How much embarrassment do you feel when walking up to a stranger in efforts to become friends with him/her? Does it feel like there is a barrier? In most cases yes. To succeed in opening the door to a friendship with that person, you are likely figuring out a way, a clever path or tactic, or perhaps thinking of some unique subject to talk with him/her about, in order to break the ice and open that door. Well, it shouldn't have to be that way, and it shouldn't be so difficult. Instead it should be very straightforward. For a truly advanced and ideal society, it isn't that way, and there are no barriers.

Personally, I believe in life on other worlds throughout the galaxy and the universe. I even believe there are many worlds with humans or at least human like beings. Many of them are certainly more advanced than we are on this world, and I'm sure their culture is more ideal and more welcoming to friendships.

I must admit that there are many times through my life that I have seen someone with whom I immediately felt a yearning desire to be friends, but for social cues and barriers that exist in our human society, I have not been able to walk up to the person. I couldn't figure out a path or tactic, you might say. I couldn't figure out a subject to talk about. I lost the opportunity, the potential friendship lost forever. Granted, in some cases, I was able to think of something fast enough. I managed to open those doors, and we actually became friends. Also, in a few cases where I had lost the opportunity, I was given a second chance, as you'll read in some of the following topics. For those recoveries, I am grateful.

As our society advances in the generations to come, we need to remove these social barriers and remove the pigeonholes that presently exist. Lost opportunities are occurring to a lot of people in this world, and I'm sure some of those opportunities and potential friendships would have been very important to their lives. One will never know the difference for the better those friendships would have made.

Dwelling on Subjects, Repeated Thinking

Many Asperger's have a tendency to dwell on certain subjects, and so do I. If I'm thinking about something, I can think about it for quite a while, or numerous times a day. I sometimes ruminate over things and need to hash things out by talking about them several times, what others consider "over and over." Some things are hard to let go of. For example, I might be concerned or worried about a friend for various reasons or for something he/she did.

What I have noticed is that other "normal" people quickly get bored with things, especially in this day and age when nearly everyone wants action and something *new*. People quickly tire of talking about the same thing more than once, and some show impatience and anger! Many people don't concentrate on a problem long enough to figure out a solution nor to figure something out, for example why something bothers them or why something strange might have happened.

While most clinicians would quickly say the above dwelling on certain subjects counts against me, I must disagree. I have the trait of sticking to a project long enough to see it through to completion without getting bored. One example is the Ford LTD station wagon project. The work I did on that LTD was laborious and tedious, and most people wouldn't have bothered. The same is true with my writing novels. A lot of people like to rush through the reading of a novel, but the truth is when I *write* a novel, I cannot "speed read" through it. I have to read it the same slow pace that I write or type it, and while it's tedious work, a lot of potentially great writers or would-be writers don't have the patience to stay with a story and write it in what to them is slow motion. To them, writing a novel is very boring because it is too slow for them. I have seen a lot of people begin great novels and then peter out for the sake of boredom, and once it's set down, they can never seem to pick it back up.

In my case, I can. I can set the beginnings of a novel down for quite a while, months, then pick it back up, and carry on writing it. As I can think about subjects numerous times *without* being bored, my repeated thinking about some of the same things allows my mind deeper access to more ideas pertaining to those subjects, and things that I initially cannot figure out do get figured out with repeated tenacious thoughts.

For example, I even have the perception to figure out scenarios and conversations that go on behind my back, if I think about them long enough. This is helpful in arriving at conclusions or reasons why certain people have behaved strangely to me or have wronged me in some way in the past. Mysterious behavior does annoy me, and I can usually resolve the mystery by dwelling on it and thinking about it long enough to figure it out, after which I can release it and move on.

What this comes to is that it's perfectly all right to dwell on the same subjects, although annoyingly boring to some of the "normal" people, and I have repeated benefit from my trait, instead of hindrance.

Attraction Forces, Getting What I Desire

In past years, up until I was 27 or so, I used to be able to attract certain situations to me, especially concerning desires to know certain people. Since 1992, it has occurred with much less frequency than it used to. The "ability" might I say, has somewhat petered out. I attribute the phenomenon of this topic to the powers of the subconscious mind.

I remember back as early as 1st grade that I chose out who I desired to know, and almost invariably those chosen ones would become my better friends. It seems that I placed a desire in motion mentally, and unconsciously letting the "energy" do its work, my subconscious mind would . . . place those people in my life. It was like bringing paths to a junction, and it was great to know and be friends with the people I desired.

Even during my college years, the same phenomenon worked. I remember noticing one person during my third year in university. Then the next quarter, we were in the same lab class, and lo and behold, to my surprise we were thrown together as lab partners!

During my trip to Australia and New Zealand, when I was at the ticket counter before boarding my flight to New Zealand, I talked to a fellow my age who lived in Dunedin. Immediately, I had the desire to become friends with him, and after our chat, he walked down the hallway to board the plane. I boarded a few minutes later, and when looking for my assigned seat, I was pleasantly surprised that he had been assigned the seat right by mine! He was surprised, as well. We became friends, swapped addresses, and I looked him and his family up while in New Zealand. I still know them. They send me Christmas cards and calendars. I've sent them books and gifts, and I've called them every few years.

When I was travelling over in Great Britain in 1991, I was on a train one afternoon, and I was sitting across from a young fellow who looked a little familiar. After several minutes went by, he pulled out his checkbook and wrote a check to British Rail. I decided to make conversation with him by asking him about the formatting of the checks in Britain in comparison to American checks. I actually had a couple of blank checks in my wallet, and I showed him one of them. He remarked with interest, saying, "That's different." That opened the door, and as we talked about other subjects, I realized he was a friendly person indeed. We arrived at Royston, and he stepped off the train, saying, "Have a nice day."

He was already off the train, likely never to be seen again. I really wished to have become friends with him. I felt it was somehow important. I wished we had swapped addresses, but then we were only on the train together for half an hour. Then I suddenly realized that there was one saving grace in all of this. I had noticed and remembered his last name which showed up on his check. It was a rare last name. Well, resourceful as I am, I went to a library several days later, and in Great Britain, they have a long shelf with every phone book of that country. I looked in the Cambridge region, and with the help of my Great Britain road atlas, I pinpointed a listing with that last name in a small community near Royston. I wrote down the address and phone number.

Several weeks later, I was bicycling through that region, and I decided to stop by there. It was a Sunday, and he would more than likely be home. I arrived at the residence, and I cautiously knocked on the door. I felt somewhat apprehensive. Sure enough, it was answered by the same fellow I had seen on the train! A look of total surprise came across his face, and after greeting me, he asked, "How did you know where to find me?"

I explained that we had looked at each other's checks, and while doing so, I admitted that I had noticed and remembered his last name, and that the phone book helped me with the rest. We told each other our names. His name was Andrew. With ease, we started talking, and my apprehension disappeared quickly. He stepped outside where he saw my bicycle and touring gear. I showed him some of my pictures of Tennessee that I carried with me. Soon, his kind father noticed us from the backyard, and he invited me to come on through the gate and visit. We introduced ourselves, and I soon met his wife and Andrew's younger brother.

Well, I stayed for three hours, and I had a really enjoyable visit with a very nice family who enjoyed the pleasant surprise of an American turning up, who Andrew had met on the train! We even watched a TV show, *Bay Watch*, before I left. I had to leave before dark, so I could find a place to camp, and they were glad to have met me and saw me off, jokingly reminding me to ride on the left.

I felt a real sense of accomplishment at making some new friends. I still know them to this day, and I call them every few years to see how they're doing.

A year later in 1992, I saw a fellow at Sears who helped load some air conditioners on my truck. I felt like I wanted to be his friend, and I wondered how it would ever be possible to know him. Well, 6 years later, when I was looking for an artist for my second science fiction novel, I felt compelled, or instinct told me to check with somebody I knew of who worked at a corner printer. I went and asked him if he knew of an artist who could do me some drawings. He gave me a guy's name and number. I called him up, met with him, and he did an excellent job on the drawings for my novel. He was the same person I had seen at Sears 6 years earlier! When I realized it, we were both surprised!

Life is an interesting phenomenon, how people are seemingly, by some sort of destiny, placed in my life. With a few of the people I've known, there have been a surprising number of coincidences and synchronicities to occur, as well.

What all of this comes down to is that this special phenomenon, which in recent years doesn't occur as frequently, is a trait that is characteristic of many high functioning Asperger's. I have a good memory for details and events, and some say only I would have the phenomenal memory to notice and realize certain coincidences that have occurred in my life. Some of the events have occurred more than 10 years prior to my realizing their significance to certain people I have later known and been friends with. See the topic: *The Flowers in the Tree, July 11, 1986.*

In the summer of 1995, I was making copies at an office supply store in Nashville. I noticed a fellow who looked familiar. I suddenly felt a desire to be his friend, but how was I ever going to get to know someone in Nashville? What connection would there ever be? Lo and behold, a year later, I was introduced to him by a long-time friend of mine, his next-door neighbor! I was quite surprised! Read the anecdote about *The Frustrating "Friendship" with Chip*.

There are likely various reasons why my "ability" to attract certain situations to me has somewhat petered out. For one, it could possibly have to do with other-level "entities" like I refer to in my novel, *Walking Between Worlds*. However, more realistically, people are less complex and less complicated in their youth. They have a clearer mindset, but as they live more years, their minds become more cluttered with more issues, grudges, and other experiences, including learning experiences, in their lives. They make more decisions in life, and they place more conditions on how they go about getting what they want. As a result, the process becomes more difficult. All of these add up and create "clutter" which somewhat interferes with the ability of the mind, including the subconscious, to go about setting up important situations and synchronicities in their lives.

This "clutter" can also be compared to vortices in a river. Vortices have remarkable stability. Opinions, beliefs, and conditions, like vortices, are also remarkably stable. These vortices can be detrimental to human spiritual growth, and they can also hinder the abilities of people to attract certain situations to them.

There are some people who know how to dump this kind of clutter, to clear the vortices, so that the subconscious mind can work more freely and unhindered. They are the ones who have better luck, due to their ability to create reality for themselves, and they are able to bring paths to a junction. They are the ones who have the knack in getting what they want, including the friends they desire.

Looking Up Old Friends, Resourcefulness

Since I've been alive, I have always had the desire to keep up with old friends, a good trait indeed. I have always been resourceful, and knowing how my parents send out some 200 Christmas greetings every year, I naturally picked up the habit of looking up and keeping up with old friends. Plus, since I like to travel, I consider it important to keep in touch with people out of state and even out of the country. As I mentioned in *Keeping Detailed Records*, I have a complete list of addresses and phone numbers of people and friends who I know. I even consider keeping in touch with them so important that I have

Xerox copies of all that data in another building, the same way I have genealogical information stored, so that it *won't* get lost. Not only that, I have all the university student directories for the years I went to school. Many of the student listings also give the parents' home address. That has proven very helpful in looking up some friends of mine several years later, especially those that only went to that school for a year or two and are therefore not in the alumni directory.

Of course, I have looked up many old friends, which means they have heard from me out of the clear blue. It would literally take me a thousand years to hear from people out of the clear blue as many times as others combined have heard from me. Many of them are glad to hear from me, but in more recent years, I have discovered that some of them have become a little bit evasive. Some have thought I was strange, and some have even slightly resented it! Part of the reason is the increase in general paranoia in society.

Of course, my looking them up is always with the good intention of enjoying the visit or doing activities with them. As time goes on, I have observed that it is more difficult to keep in touch because nearly 100% of my friends leave it up to me to contact them. Plus, if they move or get an unlisted phone number, I lose contact with them. I like to be able to call them on the telephone because if I write them, I usually don't hear from them. At least on the telephone, we have two-way communication *during* the phone conversation. By mail or email, communication is almost always one way, from me to them. I have to admit that with most of my friends, I feel like we have a one-way bridge.

I know for a fact that there are several friends I have who, to look them up, I have to go through their parents. This is necessary especially for the few I know in the military service, and also true for others who have unlisted phone numbers. Not all parents are accommodating either, for lack of trust or simply not knowing me, which adds to the difficulty! For those parents who have accommodated me, I am grateful, but I know that when they die in the future, I will lose contact with their children, who are my friends. I won't have any avenue to reach them anymore, and I know that I will be sorry to lose them. Plus, I doubt it will ever occur to them to contact me during the rest of our lives. It's just not that important to them. One mother was so unaccommodating and non-responsive that I marched myself right over to the Register of Deeds and secured the deed information (therefore his address) for one friend of mine and I found him! Deed information is public, and it's available to anyone. While there are unlisted phone numbers, there are *no* unlisted deeds.

To do with resourcefulness, as a side note, I have observed that other people don't take the time to open and review their bank statements, their phone bills, their insurance policies, or other important documents and itemizing. They check it barely long enough to see how much the bill is, and they simply pay it without reviewing it. Well, I've always made a practice of opening up my bills and checking through all the details. It doesn't take but a few minutes. I used to think everyone else did the same. How could they not? That's why a lot of people get ripped off.

I have also observed that most people don't take the time or effort to keep up with others, much less keep a list of the addresses of their friends. They don't seem to be organized enough. This is especially true in Latin America, where I have had great difficulty in keeping up with friends, especially those that live in larger cities, like Monterrey, plus those that move on up to Texas to live.

To state one example from Mexico, the mother of one good friend of mine wasn't up to date enough to ever give me the correct and recent phone number of where her son was living in Texas. Instead she kept giving me the previous expired (disconnected) phone numbers! Well, I later found out that it had to do with lack of trust of the mother, and when I did, it rightfully irritated me enough that I went to the neighbor's house, and I secured that number from their phone bill. It was sneaky of me, but I'm also proud of my resourcefulness and for jumping her hurdle! This strange story is revealed in detail in my novel: *Walking Between Worlds*. And that's another thing about many Latinos. Most of them change their phone numbers every year, no matter what, and to add to the difficulty, their phone numbers are unlisted. I guess they do have some reason, to avoid being caught up with by U.S. Immigration

To state another example from Mexico, one other friend of mine moved off to Texas just last year, and I wanted to look him up either going to or coming back from Mexico. Even though I stayed in Bustamante and the area for over a month, his mother never did get it together to secure the phone number of her cousins in Texas, where her son was living. I was surprised she never had the number in the first place, and after the month went by, I proceeded to ask her the obvious question of, *If you all had an emergency here in Mexico, how in the world would you let your son know?* She said she has an aunt in Monterrey who has the number of her cousin. I asked her if she would be willing to call him through her aunt, because I was only going to be in town another week before driving back to Tennessee. She didn't do it. You see, phone calls are very expensive in Mexico, especially when calling the USA. So, that's part of the reason Mexicans don't always have phone numbers of their Texas relatives. Emergency calls are worth the expense, but nothing less urgent.

I must admit it gets very frustrating the lack of resourcefulness and the lack of trust of other people, all which makes me work that much harder, out of spite, to get the information and find what I want. I mean really, all I want to do is enjoy knowing my friends. I'm not a threat. Plus, it's not that hard to be resourceful, and I always thought that being better organized was a better trait than not. I wish people would see it as more important to keep up with their friends, like I do. People need to trust each other more than they do. If they would quit being so paranoid, there would be far fewer problems in this world.

Expecting Friendships to Continue

Several years ago, a friend told me, "You know, Robert, when someone is nice to you, you expect it to continue, but unfortunately that's not always the case." Right he is. He also told me that if a person sees a stranger who looks friendly, then he ought to be able to walk right up to him, tell him he likes him, and become friends. That should be an acceptable norm in society.

From day one, I have always been a person to appreciate friendships and to sincerely appreciate those who are my friends. As I live my life, I have noticed that a lot of friends come and go. For some friends of mine, I just don't have enough assurance that they are indeed my friends, and assurance is something that I need. Some people say that for your whole lifetime, you can count your friends on one hand. Well, I won't be that extreme to say that, but I will admit that a lot of friendships are just temporary and your really good friends are just a small percentage of the lot.

As I have the trait of resisting change, I naturally expect things to continue. Friendships are one of those things. I've made a lot of friends in life, and I like to keep up with them. When travelling I swap addresses with people I meet along the way. When I was in university, I made plenty of friends, and after graduating, I have made efforts to keep up with them. However, I have heard (out of the clear blue) from only 4 of them since graduating in 1991.

Each Christmas, I have been known to send from 50 to 100 Season's Greetings, and I used to have the positive expectation that I would hear from them and swap Christmas greetings with them year after year, like my parents do every year. Well, I only heard back from a very few. In more recent years, I have gotten away from sending out so many greetings because I just don't hear from them. However, there are a few who write back, and subsequently send me a greeting with a thanks for staying in touch. So, out of the lot, I always find a few good ones.

Since I graduated from university in 1991, I have found that it has been more difficult to make new friends. While I have made a few good friends, and I am grateful for that much, I have to admit that I find it appalling how many new friendships were only temporary and have fallen to the wayside. Now granted, many of them were cases of just drifting apart, which I consider an acceptable norm, but there are also some that have ended for their resentment or anger or even hatred toward me. While I've had falling outs with some new friends in this country and also in other nations, the majority of those falling outs have occurred in Mexico. A selected few of those rejections have been *worse* than just annoying to me.

Now don't get me wrong. Mexico does have a lot of great people, and I have indeed made some good friends in that country during the past ten years. Some of us have done things together, gone up in the mountains, and visited different places of interest.

We have to be taught and we have to learn to realize that not all people are true friends. It's difficult to discern who is and who isn't a friend. Even when genuinely paying attention to your inner feelings, it is still very tricky, and deception is unfortunately all too easy. Learning how to discern is an art in itself that not everyone has. It's like an instinct to recognize or feel out a friendship. I believe my instincts lacked development in that area. For a few "friends" I've had, (and sorry but this pertains to Mexico) maintaining my friendships with them was like navigating a mine field without road signs!

Of all the friends I've ever made, I have never done anything with the intent of severing a friendship. It's not my nature to sever friendships. Even though I treat them nicely and I'm considerate, the number of mysterious rejections I have suffered, since graduating from university, do indeed exceed the number I would have expected. As a result, it's been very difficult for me to depend on who my true friends really are. I don't think it's just me either. I think many people have suffered rejections.

Detailed accounts of several good friendships, along with analyses, can be read in my novel: *Walking Between Worlds*.

I know and realize that in a few of those cases, my idiosyncrasies and intolerance of smoke and perfume has caused some of my friendships to come to an end, but that's certainly not the case for all of them. I do have high standards, and I expect to be treated with respect by my friends, and some of those who have taken a dislike to me have told me that I'm pushy or intolerant.

While staying with families, I have tolerated quite a bit, especially from people smoking and perfuming themselves, up to several times a day, in their own homes! I have always asked nicely and explained that smoke and perfume bother me. Some have accommodated me, but others have been very defensive, hostile, and angry about it! It all depends on how much they want my friendship, doesn't it. That's what I have come to realize.

I also have enough sense to realize that some of my friendships have been friendships of convenience, to them! More than the usual share of that has occurred in Mexico, as one will read in my novel. I have been taken advantage of several times, for my unassuming and unsuspecting nature, and a lot of people have mysteriously avoided saying the words "thank you" or "gracias".

I view friendships as one would view a friendship with a dog. Dogs either like you or dislike you, and almost 100% of the time, it stays that way. Once a friend, always a friend. Why can't all humans be as loyal and friendly to each other as a dog? Granted, there are a few unpredictable dogs out there in the world, but the percentage in humans is much higher.

Nevertheless, whenever I make a new friend, I have good feelings, and I naturally take it for granted that it will last for a lifetime. That's always my preconception and my positive way of thinking. At least for some friends I've made in life, it really is this way. I recognize and appreciate those who are my true friends and that they happily greet me each time I look them up.

I have lifted an excerpt out of my novel: *Walking Between Worlds* about coming on too strong. Here it is.

*   *   *

Roland talked with Lorenzo and Glenda about people in general, and they thought Roland was coming on too strong, that he was going over to Leonardo's house too much and might be coming across as pushy. Well, Roland didn't think that was true. Leonardo was repeatedly not at home, and Roland had to go by there more than once to have any chance of finding him at home. Plus, he was just going about the normal maneuvers to succeed in making plans about going up in the mountains with Leonardo and camping. They also said to Roland that he was stubborn. Yes, that was true. When Roland set some goals for himself and possibly with others, he did whatever was necessary to accomplish them. To him, his maneuvers were reasonable in nature, even if others didn't agree with that.

*   *   *

One can see the characteristics of an Asperger's, the way Roland was persistent in "going over there too much," even though he didn't agree with that.

To add a positive note to this topic, about Leonardo, I still know him, and I average seeing him about once a year. That is, I happen to catch him at home. We catch up with each other and what we are doing, and he still shows an interest in being a friend. He even gave me his new address in Monterrey the last time I saw him, telling me to look him up in the future.

While in Mexico, I actually enjoy going around town and visiting people who are my friends. After all, having friends is important, and it's something I enjoy.

High Expectations of Behavior

Someone also told me that I expect people to be better than they actually are. That is very true, and it's not something to be ashamed of. I do indeed expect people to be on good behavior. Like I mentioned in the previous topic, I have high standards, and I expect to be treated with respect by my friends. While some people are very good about that, others aren't. Some people have a natural tendency to behave badly and according to low standards, and when they're around me, they are uncomfortable because they feel they have to behave better around me. As a result, they resent my expectation.

Well, we live in a society where bad behavior is tolerated less and less, compared to generations ago when civil rights and civil liberties were not even respected for certain races. Most people don't like to be mistreated, and I agree. I don't approve of bad behavior, and while my intolerance of it has cost me some friendships, I must admit that it is a relief not to know those certain abusive people anymore.

Rest assured that there are some people out there who have a natural tendency to be nice. It's not a standard that they have a tendency to behave badly, even though some people are that way. What is very important is that bad behavior is unacceptable and is not to be tolerated. People in a modern civilized society must conform enough to behave well.

Granted, many autistics and Asperger's do throw tantrums and create scenes, and I do not condone such rash behavior. While I do not want harsh punishment for them, I do believe they can be trained in various ways so that they can learn to improve and meet the norms of society.

Now, I must mention that it isn't only autistics and Asperger's who throw tantrums. There are plenty of clinically normal people who are aggressive and are tantrum throwers, even in their adulthood. For example, there was one past friend of mine in college who had a bad temper. One day there was an error with his bank account bookkeeping, and as a result he overdrew without realizing it, until the bank statement arrived in the mail. I happened to be with him when he found out, and you talk about being mad! He was like a hornet! One could say he freaked out. He ranted and raved, cussed a blue streak, and talked about how he was going to have it out with the bank president, and so on! My goodness! I know I don't do things like that. I was quite surprised! With that same person, there was another incident where I was riding with him in his car, and as he was parking, some other driver called out some comments about watching out where he was going, and the driver drove on. My friend got so angry, inordinately angry, at that man for having called out to him! I was appalled at my friend's excessive and aggressive reaction! As far as I know, this now past friend of mine was clinically normal, but he sure did have a bad temper. Thankfully, he never totally freaked out at me.

I naturally prefer to be around people who are calm, reasonable, and easy going. It's more enjoyable for me.

Derailed Good Intentions

I have observed a very strange and discouraging phenomenon in life concerning some "friends" that I have known. Several times I have kindly and innocently looked forward to looking up a friend, and I have had in my mind for several years before I actually do it, the good thoughts and intentions of visiting him/her. Many of them live out of state or even out of the country. In several cases, something goes wrong. One could say that "something gets in the water."

One example concerns a high school friend, who saw me at a ball game, and he sincerely told me to stop by and visit. I kept that good intention in mind for several years, 8 years, but I never actually went by there, even though I wanted to. Well, our 10-year high school reunion came up, and we saw each other there and caught up with each other. I recalled his invitation from 8 years ago, and a week after the reunion, I stopped by his house. Well, he was working nights, and was asleep. His mother had always been friendly for the 18 years that I had known her, but on the day I went by to look up her son, she was strangely cold shouldered, and she firmly stated that she would *not* wake him! I was put off! I tried 2 or 3 times after that to call him, and his mother, without greeting me, always answered in reference to his being there, "No he **isn't**." I never got to see him again, and all I wanted to do was enjoy and continue my friendship with someone I knew back in school. Perhaps she thought I was gay to look up friends after the reunion, or that I was strange to do so. If that's what she really thought, then she's pathetic! What I do know is that she resented my kindly looking up her son!

I met a fellow named Chris while I was in Australia in 1990. We became good friends on the spot, and during the next 4 years, he wrote me repeated letters of coming over to visit him, that we could do some hiking and travelling. He moved to Europe and then to England and continued to write. In 1993, I invited him to come over so we could go to California and hike the John Muir Trail. He said he would really like to but never actually came. Finally in 1994, I had the chance to fly to England, where I was glad to look him up. Well, he had just gotten a girlfriend who he was totally in love with, and it was a whole different kettle of fish, as a result! It frustrated me that he was strangely cold shouldered and was always rushing out the door to see his girlfriend. We had a disagreement about taking me to the airport, which severed our friendship! I also believe he was intimidated by my phenomenal memory, because I was innocently remembering all of our conversations from 4 years ago. It's now been 12 years, and I still remember all of the conversations! It's a long story. See my novel: *Walking Between Worlds.*

Another classic example is when I went to look up a college friend in Austin, Texas. Back in school he was a good friend, but when I looked him up 10 years later, he was cautious and his face kept going cold every few minutes with an expression of, *Who is this guy?! What does he want?* I had wanted to stop through overnight, but he told me he didn't know me that well, and he kept acting like he didn't remember me. Maybe he really didn't, which is hard for me to believe, but something was strangely cold in his eyes! I never looked him up again.

Another case involves my sincere appreciation for some "friends" in Miami, Florida, who I had visited in 1990 and 1995. I wanted to return to visit again, and I looked forward to the time when I would finally do so. Well, I drove down there and visited for a 3-day weekend just last year, 2001, and even though I truly behaved myself very well and was enjoying my time with them, I was suddenly and surprisingly rejected by two members in that family in less than 48 hours! The "friend" who was my age even had the audacity to tell me, "Robert, your coming down here and asking to stay with my family sets up an excellent chance for rejection." *Whew!* What an awful comment! My "wearing out my welcome" that fast just didn't make any sense. I was appalled, to say the least!

I could go on. There are several more stories. The main point is that many of my innocent and good intentions have, for strange reasons, been frustratingly derailed, and I have to admit that I have somewhat lost my desire to look up old friends. To speculate, this discouraging phenomenon likely occurs due to my good intentions and thoughts of looking forward to visiting with them being unconsciously picked up by them in their sleep, likely resulting in dreams that scare them off. It's like they're receiving a telepathic forewarning from me, as if I'm a threat, which I know I'm not. Is it that, or does it have to do with other-level "entities" such as the ones in my novel, *Walking Between Worlds*, sending dreams to my friends with the mission of ruining friendships?

No matter what, this phenomenon should not be a reality, and it has no place in society! Rejections do not belong in our lives. Instead of setting up excellent chances for rejection, all of us need to clear out our "clutter" and then set up excellent chances for compensation, that is, excellent chances for *good* and *friendly* compensation. Better yet, let's say excellent chances for *acceptance*.

As a commentary, I want to ask the reader, *How many times do you hear from an old friend out of the clear blue?* Likely very rarely. For me, I average hearing from one or two a year. Some years I don't hear from anyone at all. Almost everybody I know leaves it up to me to contact them. I don't think it's just me. I think this happens to most everyone.

People are not used to looking up old friends, and it really bothers me that it is not in our culture to do so. For many people, it feels strangely abnormal to look up old friends, for lack of cultural training! We are never taught as children to look up friends; therefore we never learn the habit and never do so when we are adults! That is something that society needs to add to its agenda, to train people in childhood to *look up* their friends. If that were done, there would be a lot less strange reactions when being looked up by people like me. After all, having friends is very important in life.

In more recent years, there are web sites about Personals and Dating services that flash up their announcements on screen periodically. Some of them offer services of looking up old high school friends, and they offer ways of finding them. Another announcement offers services of placing personal ads, and services of finding people of similar interests and making new friends. These services are encouraging. Maybe after another generation, things will improve and society will become more social in that aspect. I will certainly welcome that.

Now don't think I have forgotten about all those who *are* my friends. To add a more positive note to this topic, I recently looked up a family I hadn't seen for 18 years, and they were glad to see me, welcoming me into their house to visit. They even thanked me for stopping by, and it was great to see them.

Also, in 1994, I befriended an 18-year-old fellow for two days while hiking in Great Britain, and I later received a kind letter from his mother who wrote, "Thank you for your kindnesses to my son."

Mysterious Avoidance by "Friends"

In more recent times, during the past decade, since graduating from university, there have been increasing cases of people taking a mysterious avoidance, even after becoming good friends of mine. Most of them try to keep it to themselves that they are avoiding me, but what I think is going on is that they realize that I'm a little different, and they are also intimidated by my phenomenal memory, not to mention my high level of resourcefulness. I can usually remember numerous events and conversations pertinent to the friend(s) I'm visiting with, and some but not all of them are intimidated by it. *What more does he know about me?* they likely think.

Before graduating from university, I rarely experienced a mysterious rejection, but since then, as I make more friends, it is frustratingly difficult to get a response from them, by mail and especially by e-mail.

To state one example from last year, I called and had a nice chat with one international friend of many years, someone I looked forward to visiting and going hiking with the next time I would be in his country. When I informed him that I was writing and publishing books, he said he was *definitely* going to communicate with me about book publishing. He was very interested, and when I emailed him later that week, I never ever heard from him. Subsequent emails, letters, and phone calls brought forth no response whatsoever. Without telling me why, he never responded! What on Earth happened to him? Did I do something wrong? No. I know that I never offended him. I became concerned that me might be dead. So, I telephoned his kind parents, who are accommodating by the way, and they told me he is alive and well. That much is good, but why did he suddenly "slam the door in my face" without even telling me?

To state another example, there are several people who I consider to be my friends, who I call every few years to chat with. Of course, these are people I never hear from, by the way. Some of them actually act like they are glad to hear from me, and I enjoy the chat. For a few of these types of friends, it's been somewhat of a struggle in obtaining their valid, up-to-date addresses. One of them recently, in a very clever way, gave his previous expired address and phone number, plus a false email address. I felt tricked! Therefore I have lack of assurance of his friendship. I have a funny feeling that behind my back, these types of friends don't want anything to do with me.

Lasting friendships have become frustratingly difficult to establish! To add to the difficulty, I don't always know which ones are going to remain my friends either. Some of them tell me things like, "I'll always be your friend," or, "Your friend always." At times I think I really have it made, and even some of those suddenly go strange on me!

I don't know if having the traits of a high functioning Asperger's has something to do with it. I would be inclined to think that it does. If nothing else, this more recent unfortunate phenomenon is worth mentioning in this book for Ph.D.'s to study and analyze.

I have already mentioned in *Derailed Good Intentions* that I wonder if these newer friends have had strange dreams about me and have, as a result, been afraid to know me. Are they afraid I might say things that might alter their strong convictions and belief systems? Are they feeling mysteriously bored when talking with me, even though I don't talk about arcane subjects? Are they afraid I might remember too much about them if they let themselves become close friends of mine?

These are very frustrating occurrences for me. Several topics and occurrences can also be read in exquisite detail in my 400-page novel, *Walking Between Worlds*.

Lack of Trust and its Jeopardizing Qualities

Throughout my years of life, especially when I was a teenager, there have been cases of my wanting to do activities with other teenagers who were friends of mine. I have invited them on trips and activities with me, and some of them did indeed go with me. However, in some cases, despite my good intentions, my invitations only met up with a "brick wall" due to their parents' lack of trust in me. This has occurred with less frequency in recent years, now that I am in my 30's and have very few teenage friends. However, there are a few teenagers who I still befriend, like a big brother would. With some of those, there has been a lack of trust, especially from their mothers.

To state an example, back when I was in my early 20's, I had some teenage friends who lived around 150 miles east of me, and I invited them to come and visit me some weekend. They were ready to come and wanted to come, but their mother cancelled their plans by saying no, even though she knew me and knew that I was a decent person. She just wasn't going to let them come! I guess she didn't trust me enough for them to come here on their own. Well, later on when she turned 40, her sister had some bumper stickers made stating that she was 40 years old. I proudly put one of those bumper stickers on my station wagon, and wherever I drove, my bumper made that announcement! I kept it on there for several months. That was my subtle protest against her and her decision! I also took a picture of the back of my car, and I mailed it to her, along with a note telling her why.

Several years ago, a mother of a good friend of mine had lack of trust in me due to my Asperger's Syndrome traits. She was afraid of it and couldn't figure it out. Asperger's Syndrome was like a void to her, and she placed her worst fears in it, instead of trying to understand it. I speculated that behind the scenes, she was warning her son of my "dangerous characteristics" and telling him to keep his distance. I felt like she was jeopardizing my friendship with him. She even had the audacity to tell me there was no way her son was doing activities with me, unless her husband came along as a chaperone! Well, that rightfully irritated me! In addition to expressing my disapproval, I'll tell you what else I did. I called my friend on the phone, spot on the day he became 18, and I wished him a Happy Birthday. I reminded him that he was no longer under the strict jurisdiction of his parents, and I invited him to travel with me, too. His parents resented my phone call, but then I was angry at his mother's lack of trust, which is why I made sure and called him on that exact day!

These are just a few of several examples that have frustrated me! Lack of parental trust is something that really annoys me, because I know that I am a decent honest person with good intentions. I don't deserve to be mistrusted. Some people have told me not to worry about what others think of me, that it's not important. Well, I have to disagree. I believe it's *very* important to worry about what other people think of me, especially when it jeopardizes my friendships with their sons, as the above examples point out!

Issues of mistrust are unfortunate circumstances that should not be a reality in society. We are human beings, and we need to rise above this type of paranoia. We need to give *approval* to friendships instead of warning against them.

Diversion Tactics

Many people with Asperger's Syndrome are direct and very straighforward. So am I. I have been known to confront people who have had bad feelings or mistrust against me. I cut to the heart of the matter, and I do this with the intent of straightening out misunderstandings and also with the goal of winning the approval of those I confront. I am a person who needs reassurance that everything is okay. There are a few times I've been successful, but most of the time, the people I confront do not want to talk about it nor deal with it.

I have had some people turn their backs to me and ignore me, and for most of the others who would actually talk, they have avoided the issue at hand, by coughing up *other* issues. In other words, they use diversion tactics to avoid the pain of the issue at hand. This is a very clever way to keep it safe and talk about something else. They can even alter the scenario of some past issue and then use it to throw the blame on me instead!

Deep down, they know they're guilty of having bad feelings toward me, for something they've done to me, or that they've turned against me, but when I confront them, even though I'm courteous about it, they feel uncomfortable, and some of them even get angry! They don't like to admit it. For some of them, apologizing to me is a feat beyond their capabilities. Their psyche or personality does not permit them to apologize.

I must admit that it really frustrates me how many people in society are not straightforward. A lot of them don't want to talk about pertinent issues. A lot of them don't have the urge to straighten out a misunderstanding. During their childhood, their parents did not stress the importance of communication skills. As a result, they never learned that important attribute, and it is surprisingly difficult for them to reason properly, deal with problems, and solve them.

Mexico

During the past 10 years, since graduating from university, I have been going to Mexico more frequently. I have always had a desire to learn Spanish. At first I went with the goal of becoming fluent in Spanish, to be bilingual, which I have been since 1996. As I kept going, I made more friends, and I now go for other reasons, to enjoy the area, the mountains, and to do things with certain friends there.

My various stays in Mexico have been an enriching cultural experience for me, especially along the lines of how to deal better with people and to learn more about the dynamics of friends and families. Some of it has been hurtful rejection and lack of understand and compassion, but a lot of it has also been the rewards of making several friends, feeling acceptance by them, and knowing that some of them will always be glad to see me whenever I stop by to visit.

In a way, I feel like I've lived two youths, having gone to school and university where I studied Electrical Engineering, and then going to the small quaint town of Bustamante, Nuevo León and other parts of Mexico to study the dynamics of friendships, families, and people. It's like I've "gone to school" in that aspect. All of what I have learned has caused me to compile and write my novel: *Walking Between Worlds*.

Some people, who I have completed knowing in Mexico, have accused me of being like a little child, due to my naiveté, straightforwardness, persistence, and intolerance. At times, I did things that were perfectly all right, which I saw others do, and the person I tried to help got surprisingly angry at me! Two examples are charging somebody money for someone else (for a friend), and finding work for a friend. I have put detailed accounts of each in my novel for readers to enjoy.

A few past friends became very pragmatic with me and commanding in their ways (abusive), since they viewed me as a 5-year-old child, and that didn't work too well, which is why they are *past* friends. I could say the same about some of them, as well. Their childish ways and lack of compassion were totally uncalled for.

People may have the preconception that I'm incompetent, having the traits and characteristics of an Asperger's, but the truth is, might I remind the reader, that I am highly competent, capable, and am far less naive than I was in my childhood and teenage adolescence. Granted, I am unique in several ways, but then a lot of people are, aren't they? Remember, many Asperger's operate on a somewhat different set of codes.

Mexico has given me a chance to cultivate many friendships, in ways a little different than how I would have done it back home in Tennessee. I have made friends with people not in my age group. In Mexican culture, people are not usually bothered by age difference. They see you as the individual regardless of age, more so than Americans do. In other words, they take you at face value. As a result, I have felt perfectly all right becoming good friends with people up to 20 years apart from me in age. Most of them are on the younger side. At times, with some of them, I have "forgotten" all about the age difference, and I have felt just like one of them, that is, in their age group. Those are cases of good and welcoming feelings I have felt with some of the people of Mexico.

Though I don't smoke or drink at all, I have adapted myself to a degree to allow myself to be friends with those who smoke and/or drink a little bit. However, I don't cultivate friendships with heavy drinkers and heavy smokers, to avoid problems. Heavy drinkers are temperamental, and heavy smokers smoke all the time, and I don't like to be around them. Not only that, many of them are defensive.

While still in school, I had high intolerance for smokers and for those who drank, and I even still had high intolerance up through 1996. I have loosened my reigns a little bit. One fact remains. My better friends, who I will be spending time with and doing activities with, will be the straighter ones. I don't want to have to worry about when a friend is going to be sober, or that he might sneak some cigarettes along with him, or have a gnawing urge to smoke, or worse yet, secretly carry speed pills or other drugs in his pockets! With my better friends, I don't have to worry about that.

Over the past several years while spending time in Mexico, my association with the people there has caused me not to be so meticulous and precise. I have a tendency to keep everything documented and in order. I even kept detailed written accounts (stories) of my experiences pertaining to certain friendships I saw as important at the time. Of course a lot of that is good, but I believe I was a little bit extreme about it. Some of my friends used to tell me that I was *fijado*, which means being conscious of every detail, whether it be about money matters or just other things. Plus, they realized how many details I remembered about events and activities we had done together.

Being an engineer, I used to be conscious of very small matters, such as N$5 (45¢) loans, for example. I used to raise a fuss over small amounts of money that I loaned my friends down there. Mexicans loan each other money regularly, and they just forget about it, I learned. Most of the time, they don't charge each other, and they don't pay each other back either. I have learned to be more generous and helpful to them, and now if they need something, say a small loan or something reasonable, I just give it to them without expecting to be paid back. In other words, I don't charge them down to the detail anymore. This is one of the more important ways that I have "gone to school" in Mexico, and it has helped me overcome Asperger's in that aspect.

All in all, Mexico has been an excellent place to learn more about culture, and Bustamante has become like a home away from home. I like most of the people there, and over various trips, I have taken over 20 bicycles to give to people who need them. Other items I have taken and charged them at cost only. Some of those items include Cedar sawmill lumber for one of the carpentry businesses.

Obsessions and Worries

This is one trait I only recently outgrew in my 30's: obsessions and being overly worried about things, from what people would do, to whether or not friendships would continue.

Mexico and its culture have also helped me overcome my gnawing obsessions about things. I used to worry about my new friends, especially some who were still teenagers. Would they remain straight? Would they stay away from liquor and tobacco? Would they remain true and faithful friends? I kept needing that type of reassurance.

Back home in Tennessee, I also used to worry about some of my friends and what they would do. I remember one past friend, who I felt I was meant to meet. He was trying to give up smoking, and I used to worry about whether or not he would actually break the habit. For a long while, I thought he really was, but in the end, he didn't! Instead, he broke our friendship. He was one who would rather lose a friend instead of face up to his shortcomings and correct them. On the other hand, he might have considered me too nosey, pesky, and persistent. Even though I wasn't that way, and my comments to him were out of my concern for him, he resented my concern instead of appreciating it.

For having eventually lost most of those friends I used to care about and worry about, I have reduced those worries, and I'm somewhat ashamed to admit that I have taken on a more callous attitude about it. Well, I'm not that bad about it, but I don't worry about what my friends do anymore. In a way, I'm not caring, but in another way, the tension is gone, and life is flowing more easily for me now. Yes, I still value my friendships, but I've removed myself from caring and worrying so much about their downfalls.

Let's get off on a little tangent here and do some cigarette bashing! Cigarettes are the curse of society. I've had more disputes and loss of friendships due to cigarettes than anything else. I've had to endure resentment, even inquisition, because of blasted cigarettes! Many people prefer their cigarettes over their friends, and they are quite defensive about their *precious* cancer sticks! I've tested people's loyalty by asking them to stomp their pack of cigarettes, and no one has ever done it. After all, their cigarettes are better friends to them than their people friends. One friend this year just recently placed his cigarettes ahead of me. You better believe I resented it. I don't like being second rate to cigarettes!

One friend of mine from college once told me he believes smoking originated because someone tried to commit suicide. I believe he's right. Smoking has got to be the stupidest thing that people do. Smoke is not only harmful, but it smells terribly offensive and nauseating, worse than skunk odor! How can anyone in their right mind like it?! Instead, this world Earth has literally billions of smokers, and tobacco companies are licking their chops with their sinfully earned money. Every time I pull up to an intersection while driving, there is always someone smoking in at least one of the other vehicles at the intersection. In this day and age of modern technology, I am appalled that so many people are still smoking!

Some say that smoking is a great reliever of stress and/or depression, if used properly. Well, I am unable to condone such methods of stress relief. There are plenty of better ways. Smoking should have NO place among humans. I'm sure there are other more advanced human societies out there in the galaxy where there is no such thing as smoking.

Over Appreciation, Forced Indifference

As I live my life, I have always believed in wanting friendships and maintaining the friendships that I have. One of life's strange mysteries is that several of my "friends" think differently. They are bored with me and my conversations, even though I do *not* talk in monotones nor do I dwell on arcane subjects, such as talking about baseball statistics or boring train schedules, for example. Some say I repeat myself. I've seen other normal people repeat themselves more than I have done. Other "friends" don't feel right around me, because they sense I'm a little different than most. A few of them even dislike me.

(Now, granted, on the other hand, I do have some true friends who are always glad to see me and even some who enjoy my company. They're my real friends, and they truly like me.)

With some of those "friends" who I wanted to continue a friendship with, I have had to learn the painful truth that they don't want me around. Since they are bored around me and bothered by my presence, I have had to make myself be indifferent toward them. Several of them live in Mexico, but several also in the USA. One of them even had a restraining order written against me, an older woman who developed insane hatred against me.

I feel very strange, like it's not right that I am forced to be indifferent to them. I feel it's not nice of me, but that's their warped thinking for not realizing the genuine sincere friendship I give to people. I have had to learn to be indifferent, because my natural instinct is to speak to them if I see them. Instead, I have to remember and remind myself that they are on the "off" list. I have to remember to turn my back to them. It makes me feel ashamed to treat them that way, too.

With some of those "friends" who, for a while I became better friends with, it seems like if I sincerely appreciate them, or might I say overly appreciate them, they mysteriously shy away from me. So, I have to be more casual about it, to strangely think less of them, to think less about appreciating them, or it strangely inhibits the friendship! What I see as normal and what should be normal is for a person to appreciate his/her friends. In truth, it is bad and is a negative aspect of society not to appreciate and not to value your friendships.

So, I have had to become more discreet about expressing my appreciation. Some might think that I'm too intense or that I'm coming on too strong, but I don't think I'm that intense. While I consider it indifferent, even flippant to some degree, not to be able to openly express a lot of appreciation toward a friend, I have had to learn to be more sparing on expressing appreciation, or they become somewhat scared off. Strangely enough, that's what society dictates.

Perhaps some of those people who have shied away from me have complexes within themselves that don't let them properly acknowledge appreciation.

I need to add that the above phenomenon occurs exclusively with those who, for a while, became good or close friends. With those who are my more casual friends, I almost never have the above problem, likely because I don't think about them as much, and as a result, they are more easy to communicate with and do things with.

Granted, I have become good friends with some people anyway, and we have appreciation for each other, but one could make an analogy about my appreciation of being more discreet by comparing it to turning to the side, instead of facing it and appreciating head on.

I see life in the following way. I never, absolutely never intentionally do anything to others to lose a friendship, and in this world, it is absolutely appalling how many people take mysterious avoidance, develope dislikes and even hatred toward others and me. Are there nonphysical other-level "entities" behind a lot of that? That or do those people believe false truths about me? Have they come to false conclusions about me? I really wonder sometimes.

My novel: *Walking Between Worlds* portrays a lot of that, what happens on other levels, both bad and good.

One may also see *Negative Entities?* in the Appendix.

Friends, Genuine or by Destiny?

I sometimes wonder and feel like many people are *caused* by other-level "entities" or destiny, to be my friends for a temporary period of time. They are brought into my life to serve a purpose, to help me learn a lesson in life, or be a bridge to an opportunity. For the time they are my friends, they are caused to feel good around me, and they even enjoy my company. However, it is not of their own accord, not for genuine reasons, and nor for true friendship either. This is just how they are *caused* to feel. Just as soon as they serve their purpose, they suddenly exit, no longer wanting to be friends with me anymore! Even though I'm always nice to them, it's like they suddenly wake up, realize something, and away they go! I guess it would make too much sense to actually continue a good friendship with these types of friends, even though we likely met only for a temporary reason. While I believe it is true that we meet certain people in life that we need to learn from and that we, in a broader sense, create and set up these circumstances, what's the harm in continuing the friendship with them? None at all.

There are very few genuine real friends.

A lot of friendships like these that have come to an end have caused me to feel quite sad, even depressed at times. To compensate, I usually go off hiking and camping in the mountains. Some people have recommended that I take medicine. There are a lot of people who take medicine to compensate for sadness and these types of losses. Well, I do not condone the use of medicine as treatment for sadness and depression, nor have I taken any medicine for that sort of thing. There are certainly better and more wholesome ways to compensate, for example, continuing to find new friends to enjoy life with.

I am always on the lookout for new friends, to keep replenishing the supply and make up for the losses. Out of that lot, at least there will be a few of them who will become close friends, even lifelong friends. That is one of my most important quests in life, to continue making some really good friends. With the right people, you can feel really good, feel an inner sense of peace, and enjoy life.

*   *   *

PART 4

ANECDOTES & BIZARRE STORIES

This next section consists of some projects but are mostly anecdotes to do with various types of misunderstandings, of which I've had more than my share. Some of them were quite frustrating. Of course there have been plenty more incidents than what I present here, but these are some of the most bizarre ones.

The Family Photo Albums Project

I took on the task of doing a major photo album project for my four sides of the family in 1993 and 1994. I had been interested in genealogy ever since I was age 10, and I made a point of tracing my ancestry as far back as I could on all lines. I had asked my grandparents, great uncles, great aunts, and other relatives for information, and I secured quite a wealth of data, much of which would be impossible to obtain today, since most of the older ones have long since died.

After tracing my ancestry, I took on the project of compiling descendants information, some of them involving making a lot of telephone calls and dealing with people ranging from very helpful and nice to lackadaisical, hum-drum, and inhospitable.

It was in 1993 that I began to think how nice it would be to have complete compilations of all the known pertinent photos of all the family members, including ancestors, relatives, cousins, descendants, family reunions, and even photos of family homes. That way I would be able to look up all of my family relatives and see what they look like. My parents had lots of old photos, since I grew up in the same house where my great-grandparents raised their 7 children over 100 years ago. We had tin types, glass types, and many old cardboard photographs. These were original, and for many of them, there were no copies anywhere else.

I began to investigate the best way to copy them into a book compilation, and I had positive half tone pictures made of all of them at a local printer. Then I cut the half tones and pasted them to each respective page as I typed the text that went with each picture. I did photo albums for all four sides of the family, and each of the four albums turned out being over 100 pages. In addition to the pictures, I put genealogical compilations in the back, along with photo credits, and the names, addresses, and phone numbers of all the family members. The compiling process took me several hundred hours of work!

Not only did I do the compiling, I had to make trips to Georgia and North Carolina and to different areas in Tennessee, in search of pictures, and I visited *lots* of relatives.

(As a side note, before I made my trip to Atlanta in mid March 1993, it began snowing and resulted in the worst blizzard I ever saw! We were snowbound for days, as there were snowdrifts that were impassable on the driveway. This sort of thing would likely occur in January or February, but *not* in March! It was unreal at that time of year in Tennessee. Something's changing in our environment, the Greenhouse Effect among other factors for our planetary use of fossil fuels and the millions of acres of equatorial rain forests continually being slashed down!)

Anyway, I was persistent and was very thorough and meticulous with my project, and while most of my relatives were kind and accommodating and also complimentary of the project I was taking on, there were some who weren't, and I ran into a few snags.

One major snag I ran into for my persistent traits was against a cousin of my father's in North Carolina whose father is my great uncle. Since he was nearly 90, I definitely wanted to see him. Well, I drove over 500 miles to that area of North Carolina, and I stayed with his grandsons. While I was there, they called their aunt (his daughter) to make arrangements about going to see him, since he was partially under her care. She immediately declared, "Absolutely not! Tell him to go home!" That irritated me. So, I immediately called her on the phone, and I told her there was no way I was going home until I had seen her father, that he was my great uncle and a loved one too! The woman firmly told me that I had no right to see her father, that he gets upset with visitors, and she told me to just go home! When I told her how far I had driven, she told me she couldn't care less! I then proceeded to ask her to take me over there, and her answer was, "I will not!" Then she threatened me that if I went over there, she would call the police! She had recently written a couple of my relatives a very cold letter when they had requested to come over to North Carolina and see her father. I argued with her and firmly told her how hostile she was being to me, and that the letter she wrote our cousins very much upset them. She hung up on me. Later that day, I went to talk to her husband to "get permission" and he refused to accommodate me. So, because I was so upset and was so bent on seeing my great uncle, the wife of one of the grandsons took me over to the convalescent home where my great uncle was staying. Why, he was glad to see me, and he *thanked* me for stopping by. That daughter of his had lied to me! I don't know why she was such a wall of ice and so mean to me, but what I do know is that she was over protective and very possessive of her father! Actually she was way out of line. I'm glad I went to see him anyway, because he died just a few years later.

Anyway, there will always be some who detest persistent people.

As I was compiling the albums, I typed up announcement letters and sent them to all family members offering them a chance to buy my compilation and pointing out that it would be a valuable and important book for all members of the family for generations to come.

When I had completed the compiling, I searched for the best type of copying machine to copy the many pages of half tone pictures. Another cousin of my father, (and this one is a nice man), supplied me, free of charge, 20 reams (10,000 sheets) of excellent 70 lb paper. He also referred me to Xerox Business Services in Nashville. I went to talk to them, and they introduced me to the Xerox 5090 and Xerox 5390 copying machines, which they had right there on site. They were excellent machines, and they copied the half tones perfectly. For the first book in 1993, I did the copying right there at Xerox Business Services. Next, I collated the pages, GBC bound them, and sold the copies to family members at cost. I had a few of the copies hardbound, and some were done on acid free paper, as well.

The next year, 1994, Xerox Business Services no longer had their machines. So, I had to search for places of business that had that type of machine. I asked a lady at Xerox what places of business in the Nashville area, apart from Kinko's, had Xerox 5090 or 5390 machines. She called me back and gave me the name of a corner printer place of business in west Nashville, told me to call that place, and they'd be able to take care of my application. So, I called the owner of that corner printer to check on the price. I told him the type of job I needed done, weight of the paper, and how many sheets would be involved in the whole job. He told me he would have to add it up and would call me back. I said that in case I wasn't home at the time he calls to just leave it on my answering machine. Well, he suddenly got real huffy, said they're not in business to give the lowest price in town, told me to take my job somewhere else, and hung up! That angered me. I called him right back and told him I'd be glad to go somewhere else, that I didn't like the way he treated me, and if he wants customers, he needs to treat them nicely!

That wasn't the only place of business that had treated me rudely. The year before, a corner printer had gone strangely mad on me as soon as I asked if I could GBC bind some books myself. They snapped NO, told me to quit worrying them, and hung up! You can be sure I paid them a visit later that day to tell them to be nice to their customers!

I again called the lady at Xerox, told her what happened, and I asked her if there were any more places of business that use Xerox 5090 and 5390 machines. She answered by saying that she had already done enough and therefore couldn't do anything else to help me. She also said she had given me all she could. As a result, I got out the Nashville phone directory and called every printer in that city. I found AlphaGraphics. They had a Xerox 5390. In the same phone conversation, they immediately told me how much it would cost per page, and they were reasonably friendly and accommodating. I took the job to them, and they did fine work. At the end of the job, I paid them, and they thanked me for bringing them my business. I called the lady at Xerox, left her a voice mail, and I told her I'd found AlphaGraphics on my own. I also asked her why she wasn't able to and didn't bother to tell me about them in the first place? After all, they have a record of all the places of business to whom they rent their Xerox 5090 and 5390 copiers. She wasn't pleased with me at all! She called and left me a huffy voice mail that said as follows:

"This is _____ _____ with Xerox Business Services. Robert you left me a very disturbing voice message, uh, relative to the job you had produced at AlphaGraphics. The thing that concerned me most is that when I spoke with you in November, I personally gave you the names and phone numbers of the Kinko's operation both in Murfreesboro and in Nashville that had Xerox 5090's and could handle your application. I even gave you the names of the managers that run those facilities! So, I don't know if you misplaced that information, but, uh, again, this type of service is beyond the scope of my *personal* job, and I went outside the scope of *my work* to get those serial numbers and locations so that I could *help* you!! So, your message disturbed me greatly that you felt that you had not been served as a customer of Xerox."

I don't know why she thought I'd misplaced the phone numbers, because I hadn't, nor did I mention that to her. It's just that the places she told me about, apart from Kinko's, were *very* haughty and unfriendly, not to mention herself! Plus if she was so concerned that Xerox had not served me properly, why didn't she simply tell me about AlphaGraphics? One can see that she wasn't very willing to help, nor was she thorough, and her "scope" must be very narrow indeed!

As to Kinko's, I am very glad they have Xerox 5090's, and I use their services from time to time. I had received a price quote from them, and since they wouldn't give me a price break for less than 100 copies of each original, I had to keep searching. Plus, for a big print job, I needed the best price possible. I am glad I found AlphaGraphics. They gave me a price that compared more reasonably with what Xerox Business Services had charged me the year before.

All in all, most of the family members were really thrilled and said the books were a treasure to the family. They complimented me on my fine work, said it was a very unselfish thing to do, and they really appreciated me. I was very glad to accomplish the task, and most of my relatives admitted to me that they wouldn't have even dreamed of such a fine piece of work being produced, nor of being able to take on the monumental task of compiling and organizing it so thoroughly and so well, not to mention all the time and effort it took to obtain the appropriate photographs. They were impressed beyond belief.

Several of my relatives were kind enough to donate extra money to me for the project I did. Enough donations came in that I was able to just barely break even on the project costs. One of my father's first cousins, the sister of the kind cousin who donated the 20 reams of paper, donated an extra $100. I appreciate very much the support of relatives like those.

My reward was to know that those photographic images, some of them priceless, were reproduced and distributed to all family members in an organized manner in book format. Plus, it was nice to see their satisfaction and appreciation, and to also have the four different albums for my convenience in having all the family organized, both in pictures and in genealogy.

The No Bread on the Table Incident

Back in late February 1986, I stayed with a recently married couple named Jeff and Mary in the South Island of New Zealand. My parents and I had met them the previous autumn while they were staying here in Tennessee, and one afternoon and evening, we had them over and fed them a good supper. Later I went to Australia and New Zealand to travel around and enjoy the scenery.

Anyway, while staying with them, things went fine, and I hitch hiked over to Milford Sound, hiked the Routeburn Track, and then returned to Jeff and Mary to stay a couple more nights before going north. I arrived a day early, and they graciously received me.

Well, they suddenly decided to take a shower together, and they ran into the bathroom. A few minutes later, while they were showering, and I did not open the door, I asked them where something was in the house because I couldn't find what I was looking for. I then heard some grunting sounds. Then Jeff answered my question and told me where to find whatever it was I was looking for. I said thanks and went into the kitchen.

The next day, we went over to his parents' farm, and I helped him gather up debris from road grading, and then I helped him chop up old dead sheep to feed to the dogs. He also burned old dead sheep carcasses and heads in a big fire. This work I did for free. They didn't pay me.

Then we had lunch inside his parents' house, and the lunch was good. There was lamb, carrots and potatoes, and dessert of apricots and vanilla pudding. Jeff and his father were watching a cricket match on TV. Before dessert was served, I noticed there was no bread on the table, and I innocently asked Jeff for some bread.

He quickly answered, "Not for lunch there isn't."

Again, I asked, "Could I have some bread please?"

Jeff replied, "I don't think you need any bread for lunch!"

I said, "I just wanted to make a sandwich." I didn't specifically tell him I wanted to make a sandwich with the potatoes.

Jeff now crossly said, "Look, when I was at *yore* house, I ate what was put before me! I didn't ask for more!!"

Quite taken aback, I said, "Well . . . okay, but if you had asked, you would have been welcome to have it."

Jeff now ignored me and continued watching intently the cricket match that was on the TV. He had no compassion. Meanwhile, I was appalled and quite irritated at his apparent inhospitality. That didn't seem like Jeff at all. He had previously been friendly and hospitable, and I was baffled at his sudden turn against me. After all, I had been asking for bread in other houses, and my hosts gladly served it to me. I didn't see anything wrong with it.

I left Jeff and Mary the next morning. I didn't bring myself to get onto Jeff for his rudeness, but the next day, I wrote them a thank you letter, and in the letter I told him how rude he was to me and that it was uncalled for!

That was 16 years ago, and I have never heard from him since, not even a Christmas card or anything. Why didn't he have the decency of writing me back and apologizing? My parents and I later talked to a mutual friend of his, here in Tennesssee, and he too was baffled. He said, "That doesn't sound like Jeff at all."

So, I wondered for a long time, *What did I do? What got into Jeff?* Then, and it was much later, I realized that it likely stemmed from the fact that I talked to

Jeff through the closed bathroom door, while he and Mary were showering together, and even though I never opened the door, he must have resented me considerably. As it turned out, I invaded their privacy, even though it was with no bad intent, and that "invasion" therefore interrupted his moment of *ecstasy* with his wife!

I must state that a lot of people are very intolerant, and it is appalling to me how they sever a friendship over very small things. While it turned out to be a mistake that I talked to Jeff while he and Mary were showering together, what's the big deal? Why such resentment for that? I didn't open the door, and I didn't see them *doing* the act. I thought I behaved myself pretty well there, not to mention how I kept my cool at his sudden outburst of inhospitality the next day at lunch.

The Trailways-Police Incident

In May of 1983 when I was 17, I was on the way to Monterrey, Nuevo León, Mexico to visit and stay with the family of an exchange student who had gone to my school the year before. He had been in some of my classes with me. My Spanish teacher was sending me down there, and I was looking forward to my stay. This would be a great opportunity to practice my Spanish and make some friends in Mexico.

It was a two-day trip by Trailways bus, and I arrived in Dallas near midnight the first night. I stayed with my cousins in Dallas for two nights, and Joe Gray came to pick me up from the Trailways bus station.

Once the bus pulled in to the terminal and I got off the bus, I went to the bus side to claim my baggage. They were just unloading the suitcases, and I found my suitcase quickly enough. I began to grab it, when suddenly the baggage man told me not to touch that! I told him it was my suitcase. He got real haughty with me, so I pulled out my baggage claim ticket with the matching numbers, and I said, "This is my suitcase. Look, it's got matching numbers! I'm taking it with me!" I swiftly picked it up and began to enter the station. I was a bit angry about the way I did it, too! Who was he to prevent me from claiming my suitcase?! The man was screaming some threat at me about if I didn't put it down immediately, but I kept on walking. Then I heard some woman yell, "Call the police!"

Joe Gray, who was 6' 3", showed up right at that time, and thank goodness! I walked right over to him, suitcase in hand, and I shook hands with him. Then I told him the police were on their way because I had claimed my baggage. He looked at me dumbfounded, and I responded with a similar gesture because I didn't know what the baggage man's problem was with me!

I was apprehensive and scared about what the police were going to do to me. One minute later when they arrived, Joe took up for me and talked turkey with that police officer! Joe was the taller than that officer, too.

"Now look here, officer! All Robert was doing was claiming his baggage. Since when was that a violation?!"

"Is he a relative of yours?"

"Yes, he's our cousin."

"Well, they're supposed to claim their baggage inside at the counter," the officer explained.

"How was he supposed to know that? Besides, he has the matching claim numbers," Joe pointed out.

The police officer was kinder than most officers, and he calmly explained the procedure to Joe. Then he checked my matching claim numbers. When he saw that was true, he wished us well, walked back to his car, and drove away.

Whew! I'm glad that was over with! Joe and I went to his car, and he took me to his house.

At all the bus stations I had ever been to, the standard procedure was to claim your baggage at the bus side. Never had it occurred to me to have to go *inside* to claim it at the counter! There might have been a sign posted somewhere, but then how am I supposed to know to look for that? The bus driver certainly didn't warn us!

Thank goodness Joe Gray arrived on time to pick me up. I am very grateful to him for having rescued me from the police that night.

The Greyhound Inquisition

In the autumn of 1989, I took a Greyhound bus trip to California. I boarded in Nashville, and it turned out to be the worst bus ride I ever took! In those days, smoking was still permitted in the last 3 rows of seats, which was just as bad as if it were permitted on the whole bus, with closed windows and air conditioning. I was on the way to Los Angeles in October 1989 to catch a Qantas flight to Australia.

While smoking was permitted in the back of the bus, which made the ride miserable enough, it was a serious violation for the bus driver to smoke while driving. I sat in the front of the bus to be as far away from the smoke as possible.

When I boarded in El Paso, Texas, halfway through the trip, and presented the new driver my ticket, he ripped off both the El Paso-Phoenix and the Phoenix-Los Angeles pages. I asked him why, and he said that was standard procedure. I thought that was strange. Well, once on the interstate outside of El Paso, the driver thought he was above the law, and he pulled out a cigarette (cancer stick)! As soon as I saw him do that, I asked him not to smoke. He said he was going to smoke anyway, and I reiterated my request. I even said please when I asked him not to, and I wouldn't give in. I was persistent, which I had full right to be. Finally, he pulled the bus over on the side of the Interstate, and he had his cigarette on the shoulder. When he stepped back inside, he called me a vulgar name among other comments, and he threatened me that he would take me to the police if I kept bothering him. I told him if he did that, I would have to report him for smoking on the bus. He then proceeded to smoke while driving, saying he didn't care what I thought! No one else objected either.

Well, we got to Phoenix in the wee hours of the morning, and I complained to customer service at the bus station about the driver's rudeness. They didn't show sufficient concern, and the whole time I talked to the ticket counter and customer service, I felt like they viewed me and all other passengers as incompetent and second class citizens!

We got a new bus driver in Phoenix, and he was an S.O.B. sure enough! He jumped on the bus and took off with it, not greeting us nor introducing himself to us, like normal bus drivers would have done. A few blocks into the trip, I kindly introduced myself to him, and I was telling him where I was fro . . . and he immediately jumped down my throat saying he had heard about me and that he wasn't going to mess with my %*&! With that rudeness realized, I told him to take me back to the station. He said he'd let me out in Blythe, 150 miles west of there. I again requested he take me back to the station. He rudely told me to shut up or he would let me out right there on the street side, several blocks from the station! I for the third time told him to just take me back to the station, but he ignored me and took me to Blythe anyway.

He was such an ogre and frightened me so, that I didn't confront him nor object to him when he lit several cigarettes along the way! I didn't want to be let out on the side of Interstate 10 in the middle of the Arizona desert and 50 miles from the nearest town!

When we arrived in Blythe, I got off and requested my ticket. It took him a while to find it, and while searching, he accused me of trying to ride for free! I told him I paid for my ticket fair and square, and that the previous driver, when we boarded in El Paso, had also ripped off the Phoenix-Los Angeles portion. The driver called me an idiot, and I told him that I'm not an idiot! Finally he found the ticket and gave it back to me. That's the *only* thing he did right.

I changed buses in Blythe and had a courteous driver who took me to Los Angeles.

Oh, but I was so angry at those 2 previous horrible bus drivers and their discourteous manner in which they treated me that I complained as soon as I arrived in Los Angeles. I filled out a complaint form, plus I wrote a 5-page heated letter to Greyhound Company headquarters in San Francisco, who had responsibility for the drivers on the route in question. I reported every detail I could remember, how scared I was, that I was trembling with fright, and that they broke the law with their smoking, their threats, and their scare tactics! I told them if they wanted to avoid some future class-action lawsuits, they better ban smoking entirely on their buses. I also told them to hire some truly *safe, reliable and courteous* drivers, as their sign in the front of the bus says.

My trip to Australia and New Zealand had gotten off to a really bad start! Meanwhile I went there, and my several months went just fine. I had a great trip. My parents talked with me by phone several times, and around a month after I had written Greyhound, I received an apology letter from the company executive in San Francisco, who said that he was going to instigate an intensive investigation immediately! He didn't refund me for the ticket, but he did give me a $20 coupon and said that he hoped I would give Greyhound a second chance and that they wanted to restore my faith in them.

Well, $20 was something, but that wasn't much compensation, for all the anguish I had suffered. While smoking was permitted on buses, I was never going to ride another one! That is, except in Oregon which had a state law. So, when I got back to Los Angeles from Australia, I *flew* home to Tennessee.

I wrote the Greyhound executive and thanked him for the apology and the coupon. I also wrote my congressmen letters requesting that they ban smoking on all parts of passenger buses. After all, Oregon had their state law, and California had recently banned it in 1988. So had Australia and New Zealand. Why couldn't the USA move on up to modern times and join them? Meanwhile, Greyhound suddenly banned smoking on all their buses according to their new company policy July 17, 1990, and the USA followed with a federal law that same year in December.

I believe my letters must have really made a difference. Most people, as I observed on that bus, don't bother to object, but I did! I think Greyhound actually took my letter seriously. They didn't want any lawsuit problems from passengers in the future, not to mention the smoke contamination all their drivers were receiving.

Bus Ride Compensation

In July 1990, soon after my awful experience, I did ride Greyhound again, but in the state of Oregon, which has had their state law against smoking on all buses since years ago, and the driver was great. I told him the story about what happened to me last October. When I presented him my $20 coupon, he handed it back to me and said, "Use it next time. You can have this ride on us. Sorry about what happened to you last year." Now that was kind of him.

A few days later, I dug up some tree seedlings, mostly evergreens from the Cascade Mountains of Oregon, and I carefully packaged them in a box. Instead of using the $20 coupon for passenger service in the future, I used it to send my tree seedlings home via Greyhound. I was leaving Oregon to go back home, and I knew I wasn't ever going to be riding Greyhound again, except in that state. The trees arrived home in good condition, and several of those trees lived and have grown very well.

I want to add comment that in Australia, I rode Deluxe Coach Lines and took a 15-day trip out to Western Australia and also to the central portion where Alice Springs and Ayer's Rock are. All of the bus drivers were courteous, and they had much better senses of humor than those two ogres that worked for American Greyhound.

Also, while I was in Tasmania and hitch hiking back to my car after making a hike, a kind bus driver for Morris Coach Lines out of Devonport stopped for me and offered me a lift. He was taking 20 other hikers to the same trailhead that I was returning to. That's where I had my car. As I boarded, he said, "Couldn't see you walking all that way." He put the lever in first gear, engaged the clutch, and proceeded, with me on board.

Well, the climb into Tasmania's highlands caused the engine to overheat, and he had to pull over. He needed to add water to the radiator, but the mouth of the radiator was difficult to reach, and he didn't have a funnel. No one else did either. Meanwhile, many of us stepped outside, and I began to think about a way to get water funneled into that radiator. There were plenty of Eucalyptus trees and forests in this area. Immediately the solution came to me and I picked up a curved piece of tree bark and handed it to the driver. A smile came across his face, and he told me, "You're a genius!" What a nice comment and good compensation that was indeed. That piece of tree bark made the perfect trough to direct the water right into the radiator.

Once filled, we all boarded the bus, and the driver took us to our destination. When we all stepped down, he told me my ride was free, and he thanked me very much for my original solution which got us out of strife. I told him I was glad I could do it, and I thanked him for the lift.

The Professor who Smoked in the Classroom

I am a person who has been known to speak out and object, usually where others don't. I don't object frequently, but I certainly do, if objection is due.

I remember in the winter of 1988, a year before the Greyhound inquisition, I had a clash with an engineering professor, who on the first day of class came into the classroom smoking. The second morning in the row, he did the same thing! This time I asked him not to smoke in the classroom. He told me in a flippant manner that he *is* going to smoke in the classroom, and he proceeded right on with his lecture, cigarette in one hand, chalk in the other!

I suddenly interrupted with my objection, and I said, "It is in violation of state law to smoke in the classroom."

He suddenly got real angry and shouted, "If you don't like it, there's the door!" The glare in his eyes made me think he was going to pick up something and throw it at me!

I got up and left immediately and I *never* returned to his class. I wrote a letter and reported him to the department head. I requested he be fired, and I requested another teacher for the same course. He said he could do that, but he wouldn't, because if he did, he would owe several people some favors. Well, I dropped the course and took something else. I took that engineering course the next quarter, with a different and much kinder teacher.

Many of the students remembered that event for a long time, and they were impressed by my bravery. Even three years later, I heard a student referring to that incident. He had only heard about it from others, and he was telling me about how some student had spoken out and told a professor that there was a state regulation prohibiting smoking in the classroom. I smiled and told him, "I was that person who spoke out that day. You're talking to him."

The 3 Month Job

After graduating from Tennessee Technological University in May 1991, with a degree in Electrical Engineering, I began to look for an engineering job. The job market was tight with a hiring freeze, and it took me 2½ years to finally find a job. While I was searching, I began to work for myself, doing carpentry and painting, and I also managed to take several trips and enjoy some backpacking, hiking, and camping.

Finally, in January 1994, an engineering firm, a company with 70 employees in Nashville, hired me. Things went well for a couple of months. One day, however, the executive of the company told me he expected me "to wear a shirt and tie from now on," and I didn't like that at all. Wearing a tie felt like a hangman's noose around my neck, and there was just no way I could bring myself to put one on. The shirt and pants, yes, but not the tie. For a while, I thought that no one really minded since there were numerous other employees there without ties. After all, why be more concerned about whether or not people had ties on than their performance at work?

One day, exactly three months into the job, I had a major wreck while driving down narrow two-lane State Highway 96, the highway to Franklin. I suddenly saw a car stopped to turn left in front of me, and on the rain slick road, there was no way I could stop, and I rear-ended her car at a speed of what must have been 45 mph. No one was injured, but her rear-ended car was totaled, and my white 1980 Ford LTD station wagon was badly damaged in the front.

I managed to drive my car home, called the office and said that I would not be able to come to work. Immediately, I went to a salvage yard and bought $250 worth of car parts: a fender, a hood, grill parts, and a radiator. When I got back home, I called my friend Roger Schultz, and he came and helped me repair my car. By 2 AM, we had it all fixed. We had even spray painted the replaced hood and fender white.

When I went to work the next day with my already fixed car, my boss must have thought that I lied about the wreck in the first place, and the next day, they let me go. The 90-day probationary period was up anyway, and while they never said anything about the wreck having been the reason, I instinctively sensed that was the underlying cause. When I saw the dismissal papers, I noticed the reason for leaving stated: "unsuitable for position." Well, I will somewhat admit that I was unsuitable, with my idiosyncrasies, but I believe a more appropriate term should have been: "unsuited for position," as in suits, seeing how they thought it was more important that a person dress sharp than the work they performed.

To mention car status, in the three months that I had worked there, I noticed that several of the employees had upgraded their cars. One employee had replaced his 9-year-old Honda CRX with a new black Nissan 300 ZX with $1,200 tires. Another one had replaced his Pontiac Bonneville with a brand new sleek, shiny, blue coupe, a Lincoln Continental Mark VIII. Another employee who carried a cowboy image replaced his vehicle with a new, sleek, black stepside Chevrolet pickup truck. The executive of the company must not have been satisfied with his new black, luxurious Toyota Lexus, so he bought another new black, luxurious Toyota Lexus, this time with *gold trim*. I used to watch from the upper office window as the executive would drive away to meetings in his new car. He would unconsciously touch his tie on his neck to check and make sure it was properly tight and fitted. Though the executive didn't realize it, he only had three more years to live, before a heart attack would suddenly get him.

With the above upgrading of the employees' cars, and with my car being an old station wagon needing a paint job, how could the company have tolerated having me on their work force any longer? They just could not have the appearance of that old car in their parking lot!

I thought I had made some friends at work during those three months. I used to walk around the place on breaks and talk to the other employees. One of the fellows near my age took a liking to me right away, and he realized in a positive way that I was not like the others. He had a wife and kids, and he used to give me pointers on how to fit in better. Well, after I left, I never ever heard from any of those employees again, not even the one who I thought had become my friend.

Throughout my life, it was almost always a case of my having to look up my friends to keep up with any of them at all. Very rarely did I hear from a friend of mine out of the clear blue. I have come to learn that in general, friends just don't make a practice of keeping up with each other. In fact, many of them don't even answer, that is, respond.

I was at first not pleased to have been let go. I had feelings of rejection, but then I was overjoyed at having been given three entire months of severance pay, the amount being $4,400. I already knew what I was going to do: take a trip to England and Scotland with my bicycle and backpack. I would travel around there for the summer and then return to Tennessee to begin another engineering job.

After all, there was a friend of mine, Chris, who I had met in Australia four years earlier, who was living in England, and he had repeatedly invited me to come over. So, I was really looking forward to it. (Little did I know the future of that friendship.) I immediately bought a plane ticket from British Airways, and I flew over there the next month.

(As a side note, in those days there were very few international flights that were entirely non-smoking. I was determined to fly over there and back *without* that awful cigarette smoke, and I called all the airlines. The only non-smoking flights from the USA to Great Britain were British Airways flights between Los Angeles and London, and between San Francisco and London, *none* from New York whatsoever! Well, I loaded my Ford LTD wagon, and I drove from

Tennessee to Los Angeles where I stayed with cousins a few days. I flew from there. At the end of my trip, I flew back to Los Angeles, and drove back home to Tennessee. By golly, I got it in right for a change . . . finally, an entirely non-smoking international flight, for me!)

I enjoyed my trip to Great Britain and Ireland. While I was there, I hiked for 6 days on the West Highland Way from Glasgow to Ft. William, Scotland, hiked to the top of Ben Nevis, the highest point in Britain at 4,406 feet, and hiked for another 6 days on the northern section of the Pennine Way in northern England and Scotland.

I remembered and thought about my three-month engineering job, and I was now realizing how much I had disliked it. Never was I able to pass a day at work without hearing numerous employees uttering foul language! I had detested foul language since I was age 12. It was absolutely *appalling* to me how the other employees used foul language so freely that it would certainly have offended just about anyone! I knew that was very unprofessional behavior, and since they were indeed professionals at an engineering firm, they should have acted like professionals!

I remembered the last day at work. It was pouring rain so hard that after I was dismissed, I couldn't leave the building to run to my car. I had to wait for an hour! In fact, it had been very wet the whole season, and I had lost count on how many times it had flooded! A month earlier, it had rained 12 inches in 24 hours, and the police had to close Highway 96 for three days for high water! I was so tired of the rain. At least in Great Britain it was mostly dry and sunny.

I also remembered receiving my severance paycheck from the accountant on the last day. The chief executive happened to be in the room, and I was going to say goodbye to him and thank him for having hired me. Well, the executive must have known I was standing there because he quickly walked out of the room, immediately turned the other way, and left! I was somewhat taken aback that he had not had the decency to wish me well on my last day at work. As a result, I never spoke to him. However, I did thank the accountant for the check. He wished me well and for me to have a great trip.

While walking through the town of Bellingham on the Pennine Way, I bought a postcard of the Lake District with a beautiful small lake lined by trees along its shore with mountains seen in the distance. I wrote that chief executive an anonymous short note, which I thoroughly enjoyed writing. The note said, "Glad I'm here, not there!" I laughed as I mailed it and wondered what the other employees would think of that one!

Granted the work wasn't all bad. I was grateful for the money, and there were several days that certain company representatives came to promote their products, including lighting designs, and they used to give us lunch while they gave their talk and demonstration. Most of the time they served marinated chicken, which I always took into the bathroom where I washed off the hot sauce under the faucet so I could have it plain.

There were also some things that bothered me, and I'm going to relate them now.

While smoking was prohibited in the office, it was permitted in the stairwell, on cold days, or outside on warm sunny days. Every time someone smoked in the stairway, I had to get up from my cubicle and close the door to the stairway, which always happened to be open. If that wasn't enough, every time someone smoked outside, the window on the second floor (the floor I worked on) happened to be open, and I had to go close it. One of the employees commented that I had a NOSE.

The main secretary was also a smoker, and she always wore strong perfume, putrid enough to make me nauseated! I had to keep my distance from her, except when I had to talk to her, which wasn't easily done, even though I never told her. My clothes were permeated each time, and I had to wash them before wearing them again.

If that wasn't enough, they had the radio softly playing every day, and almost always with country music, which I don't like, except for a few songs. When I work, I like it quiet, and the imposing radio was quite distracting and annoying! I had to wear earplugs to do my work. One day, when no one was looking, I managed to reach through the drop tile, and I disconnected the speaker wire to the speaker above my cubicle. Oh, what a relief! There was also a vacant office room, and I used to go in there to do my work at times. That room also had an imposing speaker, and it wasn't long before I also disconnected *that* speaker wire!

The real dispute occurred around 2 weeks before I stopped working there, when they moved most of the employees to different cubicles. Some of the cubicles had normal fluorescent lights, and some of them had gridded fluorescent lights, which didn't project as much light but also didn't glare over to the cubicles nearby. Well, they put me right by a draftsman named Tony, and they wanted me to install a grid. I needed more light than a grid would allow me to have, and I objected. Tony got angry and went to complain to our boss. I overheard the boss saying something about firing his you-know-what, saying it in a vulgar way! I sensed that the boss was referring to firing me. As it turned out, the boss took a vacation for a week.

Well, I came up with a unique solution. I insisted on not having the grid over the lights, and the next day, I cut and installed a hanging piece of cardboard on the left side of the light above my cubicle, blocking any possible glare from reaching Tony. He was impressed by my solution, and he was satisfied and thanked me. However, the following week when the boss returned from his vacation trip, he was *far* from impressed! He was quite irritated, and he said it carried a bad image for the company. They took it down on me, and I was not pleased. There was a vacant cubicle two spaces over and with normal lights, and I moved over to it, which they somehow let me do, but apart from that, I saw my boss as an unyielding man who didn't have appreciation for unique ideas, even though I was an engineer working for an engineering firm, where unique ideas are supposed to be the norm.

There's another detail that took place that likely led to my dismissal. Sometimes, other employees sent me on errands, and there was a petty cash box that the accountant used for reimbursing employees for the miles they drove. The reimbursement was supposedly done on a monthly basis, but the accountant didn't adhere to that very well. Sometimes 6 weeks would go by, and the reimbursement was done, as a result, on an erratic schedule. Well, when the reimbursement was a week overdue, I approached the accountant about it, and I kindly explained that I would like to be reimbursed for my travelling expenses on the errands I had done for the company. He got irritated and told me more than once that he didn't give a #%&!! I wrote a letter to the chief executive, who got the reimbursement discrepancy straightened out, but my being a new employee and writing a letter to them to correct a petty issue was "not kosher" on my part. One must keep in mind that I was precise in my ways, being an engineer. Instead, the company was upset at me and didn't appreciate it.

That's likely why the chief executive turned his back to me a week later and suddenly walked out of the room as the accountant was in the process of printing me the severance paycheck.

When the accountant handed me my check, I thanked him and said to him, "Sorry about our little disagreement last week."

"That's okay. Just go on over to England and bicycle. Have a good trip."

There were likely other factors that also led to my dismissal, for example, taking marinated chicken into the bathroom to wash off the hot sauce. They probably thought that was abnormal.

After being away from that place a few days, I realized how glad I was to be out of there, what with all their cussing and their imposing country music from the radio on all of us! I felt free again, almost as if I had gotten out of a prison.

All of this goes to show how a person who has been afflicted with mild Asperger's has trouble holding down a job. It also shows the intolerance and lack of compassion of engineering firms, even though engineers are known to think more literally and have more idiosyncrasies than the norm.

The Frustrating "Friendship" with Chip

The following is an anecdote that portrays how sometimes frustrating it has been for me to keep a friendship.

At the end of July 1996, I was introduced to Chip Collins, age 24, by a long time friend Roger Schultz. I recognized Chip right away. He was the familiar looking fellow who I had seen the year before at the office supply store, where I had gone and done some copying the previous year. I was glad to meet a new friend, and I welcomed the opportunity. I was quite surprised to find out that Chip was Roger's next-door neighbor! He was easy to relate to and was an energetic person with plenty of spark and enthusiasm. His name Chip was appropriate because he was indeed chipper. A week later, I went back over to the place of business to talk to him about a certain car part. Chip decided to take a break, went out into the parking lot and chatted with me for twenty minutes. He still came across as very familiar, and I didn't know why. No matter what, I knew I had made a new friend, and I had genuinely good feelings about it.

As I thought about it, I realized that there were several surprising coincidences that occurred between me and Chip, right down to his phone number bearing significance with several bizarre things, such as dialling a wrong number for a friend and its being Chip's number instead, and this was before I ever knew him! His phone number also matched our age difference as well, which quite surprised me. The coincidences were interesting to me as I analyzed them, and I wondered who on what level had set them up, and why?

Later that autumn, it turned out that the Schultz family hired me for several weeks of work to be done around their house. At around 4 PM each day, Chip would arrive home next door from his work, and I used to walk over there to casually chat and visit with him. Chip used to tell some tall tales about his wild experiences, and we had some good laughs. To me, it seemed like destiny was working in my favor. I was enjoying the opportunity, and I realized that the reason I had the several weeks of work to do at the Schultz was so that I would have the chance to become friends with Chip.

Suddenly, three months after we had become seemingly good friends, he brushed me off for no real reason. I made efforts to talk to him to find out why he had suddenly changed. Each time I went to talk to Chip, he made himself appear very busy like he didn't have time to talk. It was appalling to me how Chip had mysteriously brushed me off, and I felt frustrated and hurt by what had happened. Who knows? Perhaps Chip had a dream that scared him off.

I was wondering why so many coincidences had occurred between me and Chip, since the friendship was only a temporary one. My friendship was preceded by others, as Chip already had two other friends with whom he did things regularly. I was feeling somewhat lonely and rejected, having had considerable trouble making friends over the past several years! Many people were having trouble understanding my personality. There had been several other incidents with other friends that had somehow seemingly placed me in second position. It seemed like I was never better than second place in anyone's mind, and that disturbed me. No one seemed to have time to spend with me as far as doing activities with me and going hiking and travelling with me.

Even though I was willing to overlook it and continue my friendship with Chip, there was one thing about Chip that had really concerned me. He had told me a story about a severe incident that occurred between him and another person that made me realize his sometimes volatile character. I was surprised at Chip's story. Perhaps the brush off was for the best, for reasons of Chip's volatile nature, but since I had achieved a decent friendship with him at the start, I wanted it to continue. I kept being hopeful. After all, I was stubborn, and I had good reason. I had lost numerous friends through the decade, and I didn't want to lose any more. I made a declaration that I was going to keep my friends!

I asked a friend of my family what she thought the problem was with my friendship with Chip, and she told me, "You know what I really think it is?"

I gestured her to continue.

"I think you're coming on too strong. You've scared him off."

I somewhat agreed with her, seeing how Chip had been acting recently, but I really didn't think I had been that much out of order. Yes, I had gone to Chip several times over the past month in efforts to speak to him, but then how *else* was I supposed to do it? Still, I felt disgusted at the increasing impossibility of making and *keeping* new friends.

Chip had expressed interest in working carpentry and painting jobs, said he enjoyed doing that sort of thing. It was right about the time he brushed me off that I decided to invite him to work with me on various self-employed carpentry and painting jobs that I would find. Besides, he was stressed out and tired of his job at the office supply store and was looking for a new job. Therefore I wanted to and felt compelled to help him out. Every time I went to talk to him at the office supply store he was brushing me off, which frustrated me considerably, because I was unable to make him the business partnership offer! Every time I would call or stop by his house, he was never home or had just left! Chip was so frustratingly difficult to locate! So, resourceful as I am, I found out where one of his bosom buddies lived and attempted to look him up over there. He wasn't there either! That, I later found out, rubbed Chip the wrong way, when his friend told him about it.

Well, my stubborn persistence "paid off" because I finally did locate Chip at home in mid December, and we talked a brief few moments. While there wasn't enough time to talk about my business offer, I did ask him if I could feel free to come over and chat with him in the future. He said he didn't mind, and I felt a little more relaxed.

Well, I was in Mexico that winter. I talked to a friend of mine there in Bustamante about my "friendship" with Chip. Even though I had been brushed off by Chip, I still wished to continue being his friend, and I explained that prior to coming to Mexico, I had made several failed attempts to talk to Chip about his joining me in my self-employed business of carpentry and painting, and that it frustrated me considerably. I had already made the decision that I would like to have him working with me on various jobs because I enjoyed his company. Well, I had become fixated on it. What I decided to do was to write Chip a postcard where I would finally get to make the partnership offer. I mailed it at the first of the year.

Five months later, in May 1997, I decided to stop by Roger Schultz's house and chat with him. It was raining, and Roger was looking at and fixing his air conditioner that had quit. We ended up chatting 1 ½ hours. I brought up Chip by asking if he had talked to Chip at all this year, and Roger answered that he sees him all the time. I had gotten no response from Chip whatsoever, and I asked Roger if Chip had ever talked about me and if he got that *postcard* I had sent him from Mexico at the beginning of the year.

"Yeah he got your postcard, Robert," Roger flatly told me. Roger leveled with me and told me everything. I was impressed at how Roger remembered all of the details. He and Chip must have had a detailed discussion, right down to the fact that I had somehow found out where one of Chip's friends lived and had looked up Chip at that residence back in November. I admitted that I had done that. After all, I am remarkably resourceful, and I had been frustrated at not having found Chip in late November to make him that business offer.

Roger said Chip told him back in January, "I don't want to go work for Robert! Why is Robert coming over here so much?"

Roger said he told Chip, "Why don't you go ahead and tell Robert?"

Chip said to him, "I don't want to have to tell him." Chip wanted to be polite, not straightforward.

Obviously, Chip didn't want me to come over there and chat with him. Even Chip's friend that I had also looked up when trying to find Chip had said that he didn't want me coming over. It's just that when I had last seen Chip in December, he answered me with an answer of consent that yes, I could continue coming over. However, the truth that Roger told me did not come as a surprise to me. I suspected that was the problem, which is why I had not been over there in the last five months to talk to Chip, anyway.

Roger explained that Chip had a tight knit group of friends and that he doesn't have any room for outsiders, nor for more friends. He was also living it up, enjoying his friends and always coming in late at night.

Regardless of my not being surprised, this was more severe than I had suspected, that Chip found me *that* repulsive! I thought about it, and it irritated me, and I realized that I hadn't made very many, if any new close friends in the whole state of Tennessee since I graduated in 1991.

Well, the next day, I (and it took a good bit of courage) went to the office supply store and walked in there to confront Chip myself. I was going to clear this up! I saw Chip and gathered my thoughts before approaching him, and when I was ready to talk to him, he had disappeared. I had the copy center page him. -No response- Chip was on break. Another employee kindly entered the break room for me and told Chip that he had a visitor. The employee came back over to me and informed me that Chip had given him a weird response and would not come out to talk to me, even though he wasn't told it was I who wanted to talk to him.

Finally, after more than half an hour, Chip came out of the break room, and I saw him start moving stuff in and out of the store. I cleverly positioned myself in one of the aisles where Chip could not avoid me and would have to pass by me.

As he approached me, he called out, "What's up, Robert? What are you doing here?"

I answered, "I came over here to talk to you a couple of minutes."

He said, "I haven't got time to *talk* to you! Can't have you hanging out here, dude!"

I said, "I haven't seen you in 5 months. I figured I'd just come on over here." Chip passed by me as I said that, and I took off following him and called out to him, "I talked to Roger yesterday. You know, I didn't think it would hurt that I went over and chatted with you back in the fall when I was working at the Schultz."

Chip entered the freight room and said, "Wait up a second." He collected a parcel and returned.

I said to Chip, "You don't have to worry. I'm not coming over there anymore because I know that *you* don't want me *over* there."

He answered, "That's right! Look man, I don't mean to be a @*&# about this, but you wore out your welcome! I have my group of friends, and I don't have room or time for any more."

I quickly said, "I *know* you do!"

He continued, "I've got my own routine, and you threw a wrench in it!"

"Well I didn't know I threw a wrench in your plan!"

He then more calmly said, "I know, man."

I said, "If you didn't want me over there, Chip, you should have told me, but since I haven't been over there in 5 months anyway, it doesn't matter."

"That's cool, man. Don't worry, I'll see you over at Schultzes sometime."

"Look, I didn't want you to feel bad," I told him. "I just came over here to clear this up with you."

We were now walking toward the front of the store, and he said, "I've got 500 friends that I don't have time to do things with, so don't feel bad. Don't worry, I'll see you over at Schultzes sometime," he repeated.

I said to him, "I'm not worried about it, Chip."

He said, "Okay, that's cool."

As I left the store, Chip called out to me, "See you around, Robert."

I thought things had been cleared up and that things were now "cool." They were indeed, a very *cool* friendship, as I found out a few days later! I called up Roger, and he was quite upset that I had gone over to the office supply store and confronted Chip. He had evidently told Roger all about my "ambushing" him in one of the store's aisles. Chip was quite resentful about it, after the fact, and so was Roger, as I then found out! Roger was never the same good friend he used to be with me, from that day forward, even though he's a very intelligent and unique person who does some special projects with cars. We used to work on cars together, and he used to call me and chat with me sometimes. Never, not even once, has Roger called to chat with me nor come out to visit, since then. Still, I have chatted with Roger several times since that year, but it is always I who has to make that call, never Roger. Plus, sometimes when I've arrived to visit, Roger has purposefully brushed me off. It's not a total loss, however, because Roger has a brother who is a good friend and their parents are good friends with my family. Still, it's halfway sad that Roger and I don't do anything together anymore, all because I innocently went about what I saw as normal maneuvers to become friends with and keep a friendship with his neighbor Chip, not to mention, my efforts to help the guy by inviting him to work with me. I got no thanks whatsoever.

One can see that I was really encouraged initially by my new friendship with Chip. I welcomed it, and I enjoyed it. However I must admit that I feel like I had the rug pulled out from under me, and what is so frustrating is that I thought I had a good friendship and then it was suddenly over! This sort of example is what makes it so difficult for me to know and depend on who really are my friends in life.

I finish this anecdote with a positive comment to say that I always have high hopes and high values for friendships, and it's nice to know that at least there are some people who are more sincere about being friends and who are also more grateful.

The Redwood Tree Planting Incident

Back in 1983, my parents went to San Francisco, California and brought me back a Redwood tree burl. I placed it in water, and it rooted. It grew into a tree which has subsequently died, but I managed to root several cuttings, and I still have Redwood trees to this day. Over the years, I have given several potted trees away to friends and relatives.

When I went to stay with the Quevalo family in the small quaint town of Bustamante in northern Mexico, I decided to take one of my Redwood trees to them as a gift, hoping it would live and grow into a full-size tree in the warmer climate there.

(I have lifted an excerpt out of my novel: *Walking Between Worlds*, and I've modified it to 1st person here. For the complete story, you may refer to my novel.)

In late November 1991, I drove on down to Bustamante, and the Quevalo family graciously received me. I had stayed with them for a few days the year before, which was my first time to stay in Bustamante. My high school Spanish teacher had referred me to them and had arranged for me to stay with them. They had requested that I find them a pickup truck, which I had done, and that is what I drove down there. My plans were to spend the winter with them and become fluent in Spanish at the same time, and for the major favor of finding and bringing them a truck, I would stay with them rent free. They agreed to that.

Anyway, the Quevalos were very glad to receive the Redwood tree. They made it their Christmas tree and placed the Christ nativity scene underneath it. Also, we made an on-the-spot verbal agreement that I would plant the tree in their backyard before I would return home to Tennessee.

I stayed with them and helped them with numerous chores, and I explored the town and the area, including the mountains, which towered above the town. Things went pretty well for a while.

Well, a big disagreement arrived when I, at the end of January, stated that it was time for me to plant the Redwood tree. I had to go home because my permit expired right at the end of January, and I had to be out of Mexico by no later than that date. They then informed me of the Mexican custom that one does not take down the tree and nativity scene until February 2. Nevertheless, I insisted that I wanted to plant it, as that was the verbal agreement that we had made. Sarita, the mother in the family, angrily consented, saying, "¡Quítalo! Este no tiene abuela." Lorenzo took it down, and I took the tree to the backyard and planted it. Though I didn't realize it, I had unknowingly committed a sin worthy of being cursed a thousand times . . . in the view of the Quevalo family! According to the Catholic religion, it was of utmost importance that the tree and nativity scene remain in place until February 2 of each year, to be taken down that night with a sincere religious blessing ceremony.

Later that day, Sarita told me that I was no longer welcome to stay with them, that I would stay in a hotel the next time I would come to Bustamante! She also stated that they didn't want my type. Two of the daughters were always scowling at me. Pancho, the youngest son, wouldn't even talk to me, and he carried an angry look on his face for the rest of my stay. That really upset me because I thought Pancho had become a true friend.

Even India, Pancho's sister, who had always been friendly with me, was scowling at me each time she walked by me. I had taken her to Sabinas Hidalgo, and yes things had gone well, but that evening, I decided to buy some of her *dulces* (candy) to take back to my family in Tennessee. I asked her if she would give me a special price since I had taken her to Sabinas Hidalgo. Well, little did I realize it until later, India was quite offended, and I later found out that she accused me of *charging* her for the trip to Sabinas Hidalgo! Since when was it so bad to ask for a special price?

Later that afternoon, another one of the sisters, Lola brought my load of wet laundry to me and dumped the lot on top of me in an angry manner. I angrily responded by telling her to be nice!

I really felt hurt by the Quevalo's rejection. All I had done was plant the

Redwood tree I had given them. I was keeping to our verbal agreement. What was so bad about that? And why didn't they tell me about that February 2nd thing at the time I made the agreement with them? It really made me angry.

When I got home to Tennessee, I explained to my family how the Quevalos had turned against me, after all the help I had given them. One can see how unyielding and exacting not only I was in the situation, but also how unyielding the Quevalos were.

The Phone Call Trap

I had not returned to Bustamante for several years, but I finally decided to go there again and see if the Quevalos and I could make amends for the past. My Spanish teacher graciously told them to forgive me for the tree planting incident, which they did, at her request.

(Again, I have lifted and modified another excerpt from my novel: *Walking Between Worlds*.)

It was now January 1997, five years later, and I was spending January with the Quevalo family. I had driven my pickup truck down there. I had also become friends with another fellow named Raul, who was working for Pancho Quevalo. Raul and I had done some activities together and had even climbed the Lion's Head Mountain one Saturday.

Anyway, I wanted to stay in town a while longer, and I was thinking about going over to Raul's house to stay there, so that I wouldn't overstay at the Quevalos.

Well, on the morning of February 2nd, I was about to go over there. Two of the Quevalo sisters, Lola and Lydia, came over to me and said their mother had said that I could continue to stay until the 10th of February. They had been concerned for what Raul's family might do. I thanked them and therefore decided to stay on.

Then Lola told me that Esalina Velazco had called and asked if I could go to Monterrey and pick up some things that she wanted to send to her good friend, Isalia, my Spanish teacher in Tennessee. I didn't know if I was going to go to Monterrey, but I said I would talk to her anyway to see if I could work something out to help. Lola then told me I could use the phone this evening to call Esalina reverse charge (collect) and to make the call at 8 PM. I thanked her and made plans to call her at that time.

During the day, I did errands around town and visited friends. That afternoon, Raul was at the Quevalos working on chairs, and I visited him and the other workers. We talked about things and enjoying some laughs. Raul and I were also working on a project, repairing an old engine.

I ate supper with the Quevalos and then went to visit another friend, Oscar. We made arrangements to go hiking later in the week. Oscar had told me about *Las Piedras Azules* (The Blue Rocks) at the foot of the mountains west of Bustamante. That sounded interesting to me, and I looked forward to it.

At 8 PM, I returned to the Quevalos and went to the phone to call Esalina. I couldn't find anyone to let them know I was going to use it, and I was looking everywhere. Finally I found them in the back room on the right side of the house. They were all huddled together, saying prayers and recitations. I realized that they were blessing the Christmas tree and nativity scene before taking it down. So, that was indeed true about February 2nd, after all. I was glad to know that because I had thought they were lying to me back in 1992, when I had taken down that Redwood tree and planted it, and they had gotten so angry.

Out of courtesy, I wanted to let them know I was going to use the phone, but under the circumstances, I didn't want to interrupt them at such an *important* time to ask them if I could use the phone. For all I knew, they would be blessing the tree for *hours*, knowing how they had ranted and raved so, back in 1992. Besides, Lola had already given me full consent to use the phone. So, why should I have to ask again, anyway? With that reasoning, I went to the wall phone in the bakery, (a phone I had given them the first time I had ever come), picked up the handset, and dialled 02 for the operator. I gave her Esalina's number and called her collect.

I reached Esalina, and I told her I didn't think I would be going to Monterrey, but if I did, I could probably stop by her house and pick up the things she wanted to send to my Spanish teacher. I began to ask her how her family was doing . . .

I hadn't even been on the phone with Esalina for a minute when one of the Quevalo sisters, Olana, discovered me. Boy they got done with the blessing of their Christmas tree in a hurry! Olana had a look of shock on her face, and she angrily shouted, "¿Quién te prestó el teléfono?" (Who let you use the telephone?)

With Esalina clearly listening, and I made sure I did NOT cover the handset, I firmly told Olana, "No te preocupes. Llamé colectiva," telling her not to worry, that I called collect.

Olana stood there and waited while I finished my conversation with Esalina. Once I hung up, Olana lit into me with scolding remarks. I responded by telling Olana that Lola had given me permission this morning to come here at 8 PM and use the phone to call Esalina collect.

She didn't believe me and said, "¡No, hombre, es pura mentira!" telling me that was a lie.

I had really had enough of Olana and her *attitude*. There had been some impudent remarks from her during the past month. I firmly told her not to make me feel bad and that I didn't do anything wrong. Besides, it did not sit well with me that the Quevalos had not let me use the telephone to make direct dial calls from time to time, even though I had always offered to pay for the calls I would have made. With that said, I immediately walked off, went over to one of the sons, Lorenzo Quevalo, and I told him what happened. Lorenzo wasn't sure what to do, but he sensed that there would be some form of retaliation from the Quevalo females. I could sense that the daughters, especially Olana, never had forgiven me for the falling out that had occurred five years ago with the whole family, and that they also didn't trust me. Olana was very unsocial to me, and I had never once heard her laugh . . . at all.

I also told Lorenzo about Esalina's request, which is why I had used the phone.

After lunch the next day, Raul and I were about to do some more work on our project, which was at the Quevalos. Right after lunch I went into the back room out of everyone's sight, where I had gone each day to change into my old work clothes. Once I had changed, I left the room and went to a pole barn to gather my tools to begin work with Raul.

At that moment, while Raul and I were both standing in the pole barn, Sarita entered the back room with an angry face, and in twenty seconds, she returned to me with my clothes in her arms, and she firmly said, "Ya no cambies in ese cuarto. Voy a reportar tu comportamiento a Isalia, y ya no vas a regresar a México!" telling me never to change clothes in that room, that she was going to report my behavior to Isalia, and that as a result, I would never return to Mexico.

I quickly answered, "Isalia no me manda," telling Sarita that Isalia doesn't mandate me. I saw Sarita's face get angrier. I was really put out with the bad attitudes of the Quevalos, and I really didn't care to be considerate. I blurted out to her, "¿Por qué estás enojado? Dígame. No hice nada mal. DIGAME!!" asking her why she was angry at me, that I didn't do anything wrong, and strongly insisting that she tell me!

It was at that moment that three of the daughters came to me. Olana spoke first, answering the question for her mother, telling me that I had used the phone without permission last night. I told her again that Lola had already given me permission. Then Lola suddenly told me that she wasn't there last night, and since I had used the phone without asking her, (as if getting her permission 12 hours earlier didn't count), that was where I had made my fault.

I said to them, "¡Si sienten así, ya me voy!" telling them that since they felt that way then I would leave right away.

They gave me a gesture implying, *Good Riddance*.

I repeated my question to Sarita about why she was so angry.

With that, Olana told me to shut up or they would call the police. Then Sarita picked up a garden hoe to hit me.

I firmly told Sarita, "¡Si me pegas con el talache, ya te llevo a la policía!" telling her that if she hits me with that garden hoe, I would carry her straight to the police!

If it was possible for them to get angrier, they did. They freaked out! Pancho arrived in his truck at that moment. I walked out to intercept him and told him what had just happened. Pancho accompanied me back to the females, and after they told Pancho what I had done, Pancho meekly said he couldn't defend me. That didn't please me at all, and I went on to defend myself, explaining my reasoning, but how is that possible when you're dealing with African honeybees (the Quevalo females)?!

They were going on and on about that fact that I hadn't asked permission the second time to use the phone and that no one had loaned it to me to use last night. The Quevalos had set a trap for me about the phone call to Esalina. Though Lola said nothing of it, she had left on purpose right before 8 PM so that when I would come and make that call, I wouldn't be able to advise her, and then they could use that against me. Very clever! They had provoked the whole problem and situation so they would have a "reason" to run me off, and with this being done, I knew they were definitely not my friends.

I wasn't going to shove in their face, but now I did, and I reminded them, "¿Quién te **dió** el teléfono aparato?" asking them who had *given* them that phone instrument.

Lydia quickly answered, "¡Y te lo regresamos!" telling me that they would return it to me! She knew very well that I had given that phone to them the first time I had come.

I said I didn't want it, and I also told them I had planned to give them some money for my having stayed with them. They told me they didn't want my money.

I then walked off to see how Raul was doing with the engine.

It was at that moment that India came to me absolutely hysterical, shouting at me and telling me that she was going right to the authorities to have them remove me! I asked her to calm down, but she wasn't about to reason, as I immediately realized. I then walked with her to the police station. I told India that I had been good. She said that they were all extremely tired of me, and anger was an understatement! She said that I lacked respect for her mother and was never supposed to yell at her. I told India and made it clear to her that her mother was about to hit me with that garden hoe, and I had to defend myself. I wasn't going to take that off of anybody! Age difference had nothing to do with it.

With that said, I ran ahead of her to make sure and arrive at the police station before her so I would have time to explain to them that I hadn't done anything wrong and that a hysterical woman was on her way to complain about me.

India arrived a minute later, and she went on and on with her complaints, including lying to the police that I hadn't given them anything nor bought them any food nor given them any money for my stay. I understood most of what she said, and I knew her statements were false. I defended myself, explaining to them what I actually did and that I had indeed given them things. The police, thanks to them and their reasoning, realized that India was hysterical, and they explained to me that the Quevalos didn't want me with them anymore and that I would have to leave their residence. They suggested I go stay with Raul since he had invited me. I said I would leave with pleasure, but at the moment, Raul and I were in the middle of a project repairing that engine, on Quevalo property. The police said I had the right to stay on Quevalo property for the rest of the day, but then to load my truck with my goods, and to leave by sunset. I thanked them and left. India left the police with an angry face.

On the way back to the Quevalos, I thought to collect the keys to India's building where I had my goods stored. She was keeping a key under a can on the right side of the building, and since I thought she might take the keys and deny me access to the building and my goods, I considered my action a good precautionary move. I stepped over the fence, collected the keys, and continued back to the Quevalo's main house where Raul and I finished our work.

India looked for the keys on her way back and couldn't find them as a result. She came to me and angrily demanded the keys! I said to her that I wanted my stuff out of there first. She accompanied me over there, and while she stood outside with an angry face, I took my belongings out of her building. I stacked them outside, to be collected upon leaving. While India was outside, I placed my foot on one of the dilapidated chairs and purposefully broke one of the rungs. I also purposefully dropped one of my boxes at the exact same moment to cover up the cracking sound of the breaking rung. There! That made me feel better. How dare her that she carried me to the police! I had done very well not to go into a rage, for all that had happened. I knew the smartest thing I had done was to have gone to the police station ahead of her. It was important that the police also knew my side of the story because my side of the story was true . . . and not hers!

I was so shocked by what the Quevalos had done. At least Raul was my friend, and I appreciated him for being my friend. Raul had witnessed everything except the police visit, and we talked about it.

I also went to tell Sr. Lorenzo Quevalo what had happened, that they had run me off. He declared, "¡Válgame Dios! Sí, puedes quedar," saying, Lord help me! Yes, you can stay. He was a kind man, but since he was 90, he was unable to defend me and make the females see reason.

Just before sunset, Raul and I finished the project, and we loaded my truck. Despite their horrible behavior, I thanked the Quevalos for having had me, and the only one who wished me well was Lydia who said, "Que te vaya bien."

India told me that I lacked education for not having put the keys back in their right spot, like I was supposed to do. I never told India that I had grabbed the keys on the way back from the police station. I told her that her father said I could go on staying there if I wanted to. India said that with $3,000 dollars, I could. I knew that was ridiculous, and I gladly left the Quevalos.

The Quevalos had definitely severed any relationship with me now, and I really didn't care anymore. They were just not worth it. The Quevalos had created a new definition for the words: *running somebody off.* I was glad I was leaving. Raul and I got in my truck, and I drove us away from there. I felt true feelings of friendship and appreciation for Raul, and I sincerely told him, "Gracias a tí. Eres mi amigo," telling Raul thanks and that he is my friend. How good I felt to be leaving the Quevalos. In fact, I felt like I was going away with a gold nugget and leaving the scum behind! I felt fortunate to have some friends like Raul and his family to go and stay with.

One can see how hysterical the Quevalo family became, likely originating from a few idiosyncrasies I had and their distaste for me. The truth is, I literally behaved myself very well, and they were the ones who set the trap about the phone call.

And you know, it was 6 months later, when I was back in town visiting and staying with Raul's family, that I finally found out why the Quevalos got so angry at me for changing clothes in that room! The Quevalos had never told me why. Raul's mother explained that the Quevalos thought that my changing clothes in that room was bad, because it happened to have the Christmas nativity scene in it! Look, with all due respect to Jesus Christ, what's it going to hurt, anyway?!

The reason I changed clothes in that room was because it was the most hidden room in the house, out of sight of the others who might otherwise see me. I was being considerate. It never crossed my mind that it was lack of respect to change clothes where the Christ nativity scene was. How unreasonable of them to have gotten angry at me just for that!

Let's put it this way. Would they like me to go change my clothes out in the open, and prance around in my underwear for a while? I don't think so. Maybe they expected me to change my clothes in the bathroom instead. No, I don't think so, either! That bathroom always had a dirty floor, was unsanitary, and it usually stank to high heaven because someone had always used the bathroom five minutes earlier!

Well, believe it or not, there were some more hair-raising stories following that horrible event, as I naively did some more favors for that same family at my Spanish teacher's request, to do with two trailer cargos I took them later that year. The reader may refer to my novel: *Walking Between Worlds* to read those stories. They are long stories and are quite involved.

The Flowers in the Tree, July 11, 1986

An interesting coincidence happened to me on July 11, 1986. It was a cold, wet summer day, and I, nearly 21 at the time, was backpacking on the Pacific Crest Trail in Washington's Alpine Lakes Wilderness. I had been hiking for four days. The first three days had been warm and sunny, but yesterday had been wet and rainy.

On the second day of my hike, I had met two young fellows named Jeff and Tim from Seattle, and the three of us visited and chatted with each other at Spectacle Lake where we camped together. Jeff had hiked the Pacific Crest Trail through Alpine Lakes Wilderness with his father last year, and he recommended that I camp at Tuck Lake on the way to Stevens Pass. The next morning, Jeff, Tim and I hiked a few miles along the trail, and then we parted ways, never to see each other again.

For the next two days, I hiked alone, and I missed my new friends I had just met. I enjoyed the scenery along the way as the trail went up and down over ridges and mountain passes.

I took Jeff's suggestion and had camped last night at Tuck Lake, which was up on a mountain east of the trail. This morning, I came down the trail and saw two fellows on their way up to the same lake. They stopped and we talked a few minutes. One of them told me that earlier this morning, they had seen another fellow who looked somewhat like me. We wished each other well, and I made my way down the steep trail, rejoining the Pacific Crest Trail at a place called Deception Pass.

There, I turned right and began walking north. I knew I had 21 miles left to reach the next major road crossing, U.S. Highway 2 at Stevens Pass, Washington. I had walked probably only 150 yards when I came across a most curious thing, a bag of flowers hanging from a Fir tree. There were daisy-like flowers, Tiger Lily blooms, thistle blooms, Glacier Lilies, and other types of native flowers in the small bouquet. Also attached to the bouquet was a note from a forest ranger saying how awful it was to pick native flowers and hang them from a tree. I stood and looked at the flowers for a minute and wondered why they were put there.

I looked at my watch. It was 9:20 AM Pacific Standard Time. I knew I had miles to cover, 20.9 to be exact, so I proceeded. It was the only time I would ever see flowers purposefully placed on a tree on any of my walks and travels.

*　　*　　*

Anyway, the coincidence was revealed to me and realized by me much later, April 1997. I was camping up in the mountains of Mexico, and as I began to drift off to sleep in my tent, I thought about my friends, Raul and Rigo and their younger sister, Norma. She had recently told me her birthdate, July 11, 1986, and I was thinking about it. As I thought about that particular day, I recalled what I was doing that week. I was hiking along the Pacific Crest Trail in Alpine Lakes Wilderness in Washington. Suddenly, I was spellbound when it dawned on me what I experienced on that particular day at 9:20 AM, the moment she was born! I had seen a small bouquet of flowers posted on the trunk of a Fir tree. Lavinia had told me that her daughter Norma was born at 10:20 AM, CST, which in Mexico was one hour ahead of Washington, since Mexico did not have daylight saving time. Norma had indeed been born at the same moment I had seen those flowers!

I just couldn't believe it! Never had I thought those flowers posted on that tree had any significance, and now I knew there must have been some sort of message for *me*, but *what*? This served as some sort of verification of destiny and things being predetermined. What an impressive coincidence! Could some manifestation or parallel life of Norma have chosen who her husband was going to be right before being born, at which time she would have left a sign for me to discover at that moment and then much later figure out? I wasn't sure, but I was certainly going to put my mind to work and figure out the rest of that puzzle.

Not only that, those flowers were not posted right at Deception Pass, which was exactly 21 miles from the highway. They were posted a few hundred yards north of the pass, 20.9 miles from the next highway crossing, U.S. Highway 2. The surprising part is that I was exactly 20.9 years in age at the time, which must mean that the posting of the flowers carried an important other-level message for me.

When I went back home to Tennessee, I told my Spanish teacher about the coincidence. She was impressed to say the least, and she told me that only I would figure out something like that and have the phenomenal memory to remember the details in the first place.

Well, perhaps an Asperger's type person might be the only type of person to realize that and put two and two together.

In the several years following that, I continued to know and be friends with Raul, Rigo, Norma, and their family. While I realized the ideal potential was indeed there and predestined for Norma to be my wife, various wrenches got thrown in, and things slowly deteriorated. My friendship didn't last with that family. The whole story of my bizarre friendship with that family can be read in my novel: *Walking Between Worlds*.

To read more about coincidences, there is a topic: *Coincidences in General*, in the Appendix.

The Perfume and the Skunk Incident

While in my 30's and during my various stays in Bustamante, Nuevo León, there was a lady who was a local teacher who kindly befriended me, and we got to know each other. It was convenient to me because the people in the town noticed and ceased to think that I was "gay." Her name was Elisa, and she was 10 years older than I. She had three children: a daughter, Carinda, age 16, and two sons, Carlos, age 15, and Lalo, age 13.

Elisa was very interested in my novels that I had written. She also had a keen interest in plants and nature, and we had many conversations about them and about the mountains. I actually enjoyed knowing her. By mail, we actually exchanged some letters in English so that she could practice that language.

After having known her nearly two years, my friendship with the Zacatón family had deteriorated. Basically, I had been rejected by them, and Elisa happily welcomed me into her home, well . . . too happily, as I would soon learn.

She invited me to spend Christmas with her mother and other relatives in Monterrey, and I drove her down there. I asked her not to put on perfume, and she happily obliged by not putting on perfume. She told plenty of stories about her life and her family, and I knew she was very intelligent.

Well, a couple of days later, when we got back to her house in Bustamante, we were alone in the house. Her children had stayed with her mother in Monterrey for the holidays.

That evening, we visited and talked about things. She showed me some interesting books on plants of Mexico and also some books pertaining to culture. We watched TV for a while. I could tell that she had an increased liking for me, when compared to previous trips to Bustamante. Outside, the weather was somewhat cold with a wet drizzle. I decided to go to sleep somewhat early, since I had been up the previous night watching a long movie. I went into the bedroom and changed into my shorts.

Just as I was about to climb into bed, Elisa walked to the bedroom entrance and said, "Roberto, quiero decirte algo," telling me that she wanted to say something to me. She paused a few seconds and then said, "No, mejor no," changing her mind not to tell me, and she walked away.

Around five minutes later, she returned to the bedroom entrance. I got up out of bed and came to her. She repeated the same phrase, hesitated a few seconds, and then walked off again.

By now, this was most strange, and I suddenly felt feelings of alarm! So, I walked into the living room where she was, and I asked her if something was wrong. If she was disgusted with me for something . . ."

"No, no es eso," she said, assuring me it was nothing like that.

"¿Entonces?" I said, asking her to go ahead and tell me.

"Oh, dios mío. Oh, dios mío. ¿Cómo te puedo decir?" said Elisa, commenting the equivalent of: Oh my god. Oh my god. How can I tell you? She went silent for ten seconds, faltered some, and then said, "Quiero hacer amor contigo," telling me that she wanted to make love with me!

Oh, law woman! I thought to myself. "No, Elisa," I told her, as calmly as I could. "Eso yo no hago," telling her that was something I just didn't do. Needless to say, I was feeling quite a sense of alarm, danger actually, but I didn't know why! I explained to her that I had never married and that I was therefore a virgin, whether she wanted to believe me or not. I said I had never made love with anybody, that it was just not a concern of mine to have sex with people. Premarital sex was something I had always been against. Even though I wasn't all that religious, I was when it concerned that aspect!

Elisa was quite surprised at my turning her down. All of her hormones were up, and it was quite a considerable let down for her. I said I was sorry to turn her down, but making love was out of the question. A normal friendship was fine, but nothing more intimate. I offered to take my things and leave, if she no longer felt comfortable with my being in the house. She assured me that I could continue to stay and told me not to worry about her and her petty wishes.

Okay, so I went back to her sons' bedroom where I tried to get to sleep. It took a while. I was feeling quite nervous about the whole thing. Later she entered the bedroom in the middle of the night, and she nudged me to wake me up. I woke up immediately. She began to get in the bed with me, and she asked to sleep with me! I immediately got out of the bed, and said No. She asked again, and I repeated my answer of No. She then gave up, said she wouldn't pressure me anymore, and she returned to her bedroom.

There she wrote out a small poem in English: **The Lost Hug: It would have been tender, my heart surrender, but he was afraid, so I hugged the air.**

I didn't get much sleep that night. When I got up that morning, Elisa said to me that she wasn't ashamed for any reason that she had asked me to make love with her. She explained that she wanted to offer me the chance to experience what it was like, that is, to teach me the joys of sex. She also said she had enjoyed sexual relations with several other men during her life, and she had done those for the moment, with no conditions attached.

That's also how she had done it with her husband as well; only she had to marry him because her daughter Carinda was conceived . . . out of wedlock, that is! By him, she had two more children, her sons Carlos and Lalo. Then around 7 years ago, she left him because he was quite abusive to her. Plus, he drank a lot. She had wanted a divorce, but he refused to grant it to her, because they had three children. Even though they were separated, he called her regularly, and he supplied child support at times.

I explained that I would be glad to carry on being a friend of hers, but I didn't want any sex, and I asked her to please not ask me again. She accepted it the best she could.

In addition to my religious reasons, there were several more reasons why I wouldn't have wanted sex with Elisa. She was short and chubby. Plus, she was 10 years older, and she was prematurely grey! Her mostly grey hair, which was normally supposed to be black, was dyed a reddish-orange color! While I was fine with being a friend of hers, the thought of having sexual relations with someone of that type . . . No! I am a young fellow. I have no grey hairs, and I would have preferred someone tall, slender, and young, and with her *natural* color of dark brown or black hair.

None of that was nearly as important as the fact that she was married!

Separated, yes she was, but since her husband had never granted her their divorce, who knows what he might have done?!

Elisa continued to be friendly and accommodating, and I got to know her and her three teenagers pretty well. I noticed that she played the radio a lot, that or the TV. She *always* had something playing, not that it really bothered me that much, except that it was constant extra noise. Somewhere it came up in conversation, and she said if she didn't have the radio or TV playing, she would become tense and desperate, or that is, feel agitated. Playing the radio or TV kept her nerves calm and helped her keep her sanity. Well, to each his own, but I know I don't have to have the radio or TV playing to remain calm and sane.

Her son Carlos was now at puberty and began using perfume, and I asked her to ask him if he wouldn't spray it on himself while in the bedroom where I was staying. She obliged, and they accommodated me. During the week, I stayed at a remote ranch to write my novel, and I stayed each weekend at Elisa's house, also visiting other people around town while I was there.

Two more times during my stay that month, Elisa asked me in subtle ways if I would make love with her. I politely turned her down, and explained that I didn't do premarital sex, that I was a virgin, and that I couldn't cross the line and do it. My conscience wouldn't let me.

When I left to go home, she was sad. I did at least thank her and gave her a hug, and I drove back home to Tennessee.

I received a long letter from her explaining why she wanted sex and how her hormones were up and the rest of it. She also explained some idiosyncrasies pertinent to her family, along with some family dynamics among some of her members. I wrote her back a short letter, and she was disappointed. What she wanted was a love letter.

I went back to Bustamante in the summer, stayed there, and was in and out, most of the time staying at the remote ranch. I also took and gave her several books on trees, which she was glad to receive. Things went okay.

I returned again the following December, and Elisa proposed making love one last time. I kindly explained that I couldn't. She now realized that I couldn't be persuaded, even after a year, and she started gathering resentment toward me. After all, her obvious main concern with me was to have sex, and the complex maneuvers and motions she went through to achieve that never brought forth favorable results to her.

One day her separated husband called from Monterrey where he lived and since Elisa was outside at the moment, I answered. That ticked him off, and he rudely asked his wife Elisa, when she came to the phone, who that gringo was that was staying with her! He really drilled her, and they fought it out over the phone! It took several phone conversations because they kept hanging up on each other!

I offered to leave and return to the ranch until the next week, which I did. Her husband called her 20 times a day, bugging her about that gringo "shacking up with her."

When I returned to Elisa's house the following week, she assured me things were okay, that her husband was all talk and no play. So, I brought my things in for another couple of days.

That night, her son Carlos put on perfume to go out for the evening. He put it on in the bedroom where I stayed and walked through the entire house before going out the door. I called out, "Carlos?"

"Espérate," Elisa said, firmly telling me to wait a minute!

"Es que tu hijo . . ." I began to tell her that her son's perfume was bothersome, and I was going to ask her son if he would be so kind to put it on, once *outside* the house.

"No, Roberto. No tienes ningún derecho para . . ." Elisa immediately answered, quickly telling me I had no right to tell her son what to do, not even the right to ask him, because he was in his house. So, I asked her to tell him for me, and she explained that she wouldn't do that. I had no rights, and I would have to adapt! I didn't agree with that. I told her that guests do have some rights, and that hosts need to be more accommodating. What's more? She had initially invited me to stay with her. Elisa repeated her declaration that I had no right to tell her children what to do!

Well, that was that. Elisa was firm on her decision. I felt quite uncomfortable and detected inhospitality from her. Actually, I felt squelched and unwelcome. I didn't say any more to her, but there was an unpleasant feeling in my abdomen that wouldn't go away. Even still, I went ahead and spent the night there.

The next morning, Carlos and Lalo started school. Christmas vacation days were over now. Early that morning, they got up and got ready for school, and right before leaving, though I was still asleep in their room, Carlos sprayed himself with his putrid perfume! In ten seconds, it went right up my nostrils! Immediately I got out of bed and evacuated the bedroom and house as fast as possible! I almost vomited, and I waited outside for 20 minutes, even though it was somewhat cold that morning. I wanted to say something to Carlos, but I refrained from doing so. Elisa saw me, and she knew why I was outside, but she said nothing, nor did she show compassion. To her, what was more important was that I *not* tell her children what to do.

I packed my truck with my things. I thanked Elisa for having received me, and I returned to the remote ranch for another week.

I wasn't sure what to think of Elisa, and I was analyzing in my mind why she had suddenly cooled off. I suspected it had something to do with my having several times turned down her request to make love, but I wasn't totally sure. She had still been friendly when she continued to let me stay there, and she even let me use her washing machine, but she had gone strange as soon as I tried to ask her son not to spray that putrid perfume in the house. Yes, it was true that I had no right, in a sense. After all, it was Carlos' house, well, actually Elisa's, but then what's it going to hurt to kindly ask her son to accommodate me and respect me as a guest by not bothering me with that putrid perfume?! Elisa's declaration bothered me a lot, and I was questioning in my mind if I was even welcome with them anymore.

The next week, I returned to Elisa's house to stay a couple of days in town. Carlos and a couple of friends were watching TV. Then they went out for a while. Carlos went to his bedroom, sprayed himself with perfume, and walked through the entire house before going out the front door to leave! I became quite annoyed with the nauseating smell, and I evacuated the house for another 20 minutes!

Lalo arrived home, and he and I talked for a while. We talked about concepts and speculation from other worlds. Lalo said he believed there was life on other star systems, and we talked about some of the sightings that had taken place there in Nuevo León.

Around an hour after Carlos and his friends had left, they returned to the house. Carlos went into his bedroom, diligently sprayed himself again with his *perfume*, walked through the entire house *again*, and he and his friends left.

That was it! I would refrain no longer. I went straight out the back door, walked around the house to the street, and caught up with Carlos and his friends. I calmly and kindly explained to Carlos that I realized that it was his house, but the fact was that his putrid perfume was very bothersome, and every time he sprayed it, I had to evacuate the house for 20 minutes. Would he be so kind to do his perfuming outside the house upon leaving?

Well, Carlos got extremely angry, and he proceeded to yell at me, telling me he was going to do whatever he wanted to do in *his* house, that I had NO right to tell him anything, not even to ask him any favors! He went on to rant and rave, making various scathing remarks, including several Spanish cuss words. He told me that for my idiosyncrasies, people didn't want my friendship! Carlos then even went further to threaten me that I better not make love with his mother

Elisa, or he would call his father in Monterrey, and he would come straight to Bustamante to bust me up some! He would even search for me in Tennessee, if necessary!

I was at a loss for words for a few moments, but then I managed to say to Carlos that I had no plans to make love with Elisa. Then I firmly told Carlos that if his father were to come to Bustamante to do me harm, I would report him straight to the police!

Carlos became angrier, and he shouted more insults and threats. He definitely went overboard, and he told me he was going to the police with his buddies, right then!

I told him that would be fine. I got my things out of the house, loaded my truck, and drove straight over there!

Then I returned to the ranch to write more of my novel. I stayed there for several more days and then returned to Bustamante.

I arrived at Elisa's house, almost certain I wouldn't be welcome there anymore. Who knows what Elisa was going to say? With apprehension, I walked up to the door of her house and knocked.

She came forward from the back room, greeted me, and told me to enter and have a seat. I entered and took a seat in her front room, and we began to talk.

She was rather irritated at me for violating her rules by telling Carlos not to put on perfume in his own house. I corrected her choice of words and told her I kindly requested to her son to put on his perfume outside the house, to accommodate and respect his guest. Elisa went on to tell me that for my idiosyncrasies, people reject me, and that I was bad for having asked her son not to put on perfume. Plus, I shouldn't have reported him to the police because that makes her and her family look bad in town.

I said it was bad the way Carlos had shouted his abusive insults and scathing remarks the other evening, not to mention his threats! Plus, since Carlos said he was going to the police, he left me no other choice than to go to the police and report it!

I pointed out a comparison by presenting an analogy to Elisa. How would her son have liked it if he were staying up in Tennessee with me, and I diligently sprayed myself with skunk odor, three or four times a day, like Carlos did with perfume? Elisa skirted an answer. I went on to ask her how Carlos would like it if I sprayed myself with skunk odor early in the morning, in the same room where Carlos was still asleep? Elisa skirted the answer by commenting to me that I simply had to adapt and that I was very bad to have asked her son not to use perfume! Elisa had her blinders on! She didn't see the point, did she, nor the absurdity of what her son was doing and how I saw it.

I said I felt as welcome as a rat running around on the floor, and I also mentioned that I had wanted to wash my clothes, but I had to leave so fast that I didn't even have a chance to do so.

It was right then that Elisa mentioned to me that her washing machine had quit working, and she blamed me for breaking it by saying that I overfilled it with water! All the oil had spilled out of the machine's transmission. I defended myself and told her that the machine was working just fine when I had last used it. Perhaps her son had used it since, and it had broken then.

"¡No vas a echar la culpa a mi hijo!" Elisa shouted, firmly telling me not to blame her son.

"Pues, no vas a echar la culpa a mí, tampoco," I responded, telling Elisa not to blame me either!

Elisa said it would cost N$500 (US $50) to repair it, and she asked me if I would pay her for it. I said no, but what I could do is come over and attempt to repair it, and would she and her son be so kind to apologize to me?

Elisa flatly reiterated that I was bad to have asked her son not to use perfume, but she said she would consider the possibility of my coming over to repair the washing machine.

While I was not surprised at Elisa's turning cold, I was quite angry at her for not scolding her son, like a responsible mother, especially a school teacher, would have done. Her son had done very wrong the other night, shouting at and threatening me, and she had the audacity to back her son up! Apology was not in their vocabulary!

Elisa was that way. Whenever she had a dispute, she never made any efforts to repair it.

Later that afternoon, I took two friends of mine over to Sabinas Hidalgo with me.

Near Villaldama, there happened to be a dead skunk on the roadside. *Hmm . . .* I thought to myself as an idea entered my mind, and a mischievous smile came across my face. I pulled my truck over at the next available gravel turnout. My two passengers asked me what was the matter, and I told them what I was thinking of doing. They looked at me in surprise. No, surely not! *Yes. Yes, indeed!* I stepped down from my truck, took three plastic grocery bags I happened to have with my things, and I walked up the road. When I reached the skunk, I carefully collected it into one bag, then bagged it two more times, and I returned to my truck. There, I raised the hood, placed it next to the 6 cylinder motor, and closed the hood.

We went on to Sabinas Hidalgo and did errands, later returning to Bustamante. The skunk surprisingly didn't smell, being in three bags and under the truck's hood.

That night, once it got dark, I retrieved the skunk from under the truck's hood, and I opened the three bags. I extracted the innermost bag with the skunk in it, from the other two. Then I carefully walked down the street toward Elisa's house, tossing the two outer bags into a streetside trash can on the way. I reached her house, and making sure no one was looking, I quietly placed the skunk and bag just inside the iron gate of her patio, and I quickly walked away! It was done. Let's see how you and your *precious son* Carlos like that one, Elisa! Serves you right!

I got in my truck and returned to the remote ranch. When the rancher and his helper arrived the next morning, I told them what I had done. He told me to be careful with my pranks. Elisa might report it to the police.

A few days later, I talked to my two friends who were witnesses to my having collected the skunk off the roadside. They were quite surprised to learn that I had actually gone through with it, and we had the best laugh about it!

Little did I know it, Elisa and her two sons smelled a skunk all night long, and they had thought there was one running around in the backyard. It was a strong and putrid smell! Early the next morning on the way to school, Elisa discovered the skunk in the open plastic bag in her front patio. She was madder than a hornet!! Though she strongly suspected it was I who had left it there, she had no proof.

I have to admit I got her goat (an expression I learned at age 10) with that dead skunk I left her. The following week, I went to her house to repair the washing machine. For lack of trust on my part, I took a friend with me to be a witness in case Elisa were to go strange on me. As I was getting my tools ready, she angrily asked me if I was the one who had left that "present" at her front gate?!

I asked her, "What present?"

She really got after me and told me she was very angry at me. I laughed and I laughed, and I did it right in front of her. She quickly knew why I left it there, and she said she felt that I was ungrateful to her for her past "hospitality". No, I wasn't ungrateful for that, but for her son's outlandish behavior, I was more than ungrateful! She stated that it was her house, and I told her that it was indeed her house, and that her house was NOT my house. I told her I would be right back. I went to the corner store and bought her $12 worth of food, two sackfuls, and I also included a nice little unopened tube of rat poison . . . for her future guests! I took the sacks back to her and gave them to her, telling her that I was not a cheat.

After all, since I had no rights in her house, I felt like a rat running around on the floor! All they could think was that it was most strange for me to flee from the house every time Carlos sprayed himself with perfume.

I picked up the tools again to begin repairing the washing machine, and Elisa suddenly told me that she didn't trust me to repair it, and would I mind just paying her instead?

I answered that the only way I would pay her for what I knew I didn't break in the first place would be for her and her son to apologize and make me feel welcome in their house.

Elisa firmed up and shouted NO! She then said that she would pay for the washing machine repair . . . no problem. She got angry and made several scathing remarks, told me that I was more afraid to part with my money than to preserve a friendship. Then she proceeded to make some outlandish and scathing remarks!

My friend spoke up for me and said I was not that way, that I am a good person. Amen.

Elisa answered that's what she used to think too, and she went on to say that I was bad, followed by more poisonous comments!

What friendship?! I thought. I then told Elisa that she and her son were too proud to apologize.

Elisa told me to get out! So, I got up and walked out immediately.

That was the last time I ever went to Elisa's house. If one day, she and her son offer an apology, I will be their friend again, but without their apology, no friendship. I was quite bothered by the unfair manner in which Elisa had treated me, not to mention her son Carlos!

One can observe that Elisa and her son Carlos are classic examples of people who have a total lack of understanding for one like me with unusual? sensitivities. I put a ? after unusual because I know there are several clinically normal people who would be equally annoyed, if not *more* annoyed by Carlos' perfume! This is one case where I cannot believe that only autistics and Asperger's people would be highly sensitive to perfume.

One can also observe family dynamics and realize that Elisa is not willing to face up to her faults and lack of compassion so that she might improve herself. Instead she is too proud, and she has a superiority complex in which she thinks she is infallible. Plus, if she and her family had continued to like me and want me around, they would have accommodated me, like they did the year before, which says in itself that they no longer wanted my friendship.

Plus, Elisa was resentful to me because I wouldn't give her any sex. That's almost always the case, that once a man turns down a woman's request for sex, for her complexity of love that she feels and for her hormones, she will almost invariably take resentment toward the person. In Elisa's case, she and later her sons, became experts at it. I must admit they have green thumbs they way they cultivated and grew their resentment, which later became hatred toward me.

In the whole situation, I behaved myself very well, but like several families in Mexico, their Latin background caused flare-ups.

One can see why I'm apprehensive about becoming close friends with women in my age group. Most women (not all) seem to have this hang up and desire about about upgrading the friendship to boy-and-girlfriend status and wanting sex! I prefer normal (platonic) friendships, and at least with my male friends, I don't have to worry about their asking me for sex!

I have never seen Elisa again. She never came forth to apologize either, and neither did her son Carlos. On future trips to Bustamante, I have sometimes seen her sons on the streets. Lalo was friendly and waved, for a while, and Carlos has his usual frown. Lalo is now resentful also, his face having changed with teenage puberty and complexity. Elisa and Carlos continue to be angry about that skunk! Months later, Carlos was asking others in town who had placed that skunk in their patio!

Oh, and a fly-by-night business entrepreneur came to town for several months. In a hot flash, he became Elisa's boyfriend, and he satisfied her strongest desires, with *pleasure*. Then they had a dispute, and they broke up. Of course, Elisa made NO efforts to fix it. No siree, can't have her letting down her pride. After all, she's "infallible".

Many people would say that was a terrible thing I did to leave her that skunk, but then look at it this way. What's it going to hurt? It didn't do her any harm, and it wasn't a threat, like her son Carlos did toward me. Plus, I really enjoyed doing that prank on her. Might make her think a little bit and realize that she and her son were wrong to treat me the way they did. Plus, Elisa was so wrapped up in herself and her egotistical pride that she couldn't see the wrong she was doing. By leaving her that skunk overnight, I served what I saw as justice and was making a *statement* to get through to her so she would realize the absurdity of what she and her son did! So, that skunk served its purpose very well.

While I did intentionally upset Elisa and her family with that skunk present, I will comment that as a general rule I never did do anything to intentionally upset those "friends" gone by the wayside. They didn't understand me very well, and they're the ones who got flustered and angry at me anyway, even though I always made efforts to be considerate. Well, actually I was genuinely considerate. It's not that hard to do. Perhaps I also didn't understand some of their expectations, and while I developed my own strategies to socialize, in other words, bent over backwards, I think they needed to bend a little also . . . and just be more tolerant!

*   *   *

PART 5

FOOD ADDITIVES AND HEAVY METALS

Heavy Metal Poisoning

I think food additives and/or heavy metal poisoning cause a considerable number of cases of autism. Some behavior characteristics observed in autistics parallel that observed in people suffering from heavy metal toxicity. Brain chemistry is very important, and not only can an imbalance be caused by certain contaminants, it can also be caused by eating the wrong types of foods. I recommend that anyone who is autistic be checked for heavy metal poisoning and chemical imbalances. I have heard that more than 50% of hyperactive children with learning disabilities, who are on Ritalin® by the way, actually have heavy metal poisoning!

Chelation therapy, either oral or intravenous, can be administered to clear out excess heavy metal contaminants, such as lead, mercury, aluminum, arsenic, copper, cadmium, and other heavy metals.

Lead (Pb) is a soft malleable grey colored metal, and it causes significant health problems at relatively low exposures. It harms the human nervous system, reduces the production of red blood cells, harms the kidneys, the reproductive system, and alters behavior. It remains in the blood stream for short periods of time, and then it settles in the bones and teeth, taking the place of calcium. I believe lead also causes chronic diseases.

Lead poisoning is caused by a variety of sources. Lead was used in house paints for many years, but was banned in those products in the 1970's. Lead was used in regular gasoline in the United States until the summer of 1995, and in Mexico until the autumn of 1997. Even today, many nations still use leaded gasolines, including many nations in Europe! Burning leaded fuels in millions of automobiles spews literally millions of tons of exhaust, including lead into the atmosphere! Lead is still used in car batteries, ammunition, and lead solder. Lead poisoning is also caused by drinking water from houses where plumbing was installed using lead solder!

Mercury (Hg) is a heavy, silver/white liquid at room temperature. It is very toxic indeed, more so than lead. Mercury is used in thermometers, pesticides, pharmaceutical preparations, some dental fillings, and certain switches and lamps. Mercury poisoning and autism have remarkably similar symptoms, such as: self injurious behavior, social withdrawal, lack of eye contact and facial expressions, repetitive behaviors, and hypersensitivity to certain noises and touch.

One of the main sources of exposure (which causes poisoning) comes from mercury amalgam tooth fillings, which, as far as I'm concerned should never be installed by dentists! There are other materials such as white composite that work very well and are NOT poisonous. While OSHA has classified dental amalgam as toxic waste, the American Dental Association thinks differently, that mercury amalgam is perfectly safe while it is in your mouth, and also in the mouths of children! This causes an on-going and constant source of exposure 24 hours a day, 365 days a year, due to chewing and the fact that mercury vapor leaks continually from the fillings. Recognizing how toxic mercury really is, the practice of installing mercury amalgam dental fillings is atrocious to say the least! Mercury has NO place in our mouths.

Mercury poisoning also comes, seriously, from pharmaceutical shots and vaccines! Thimerosal is a mercury containing preservative in many shots. That also is atrocious to say the least!

Aluminum (Al) is the third most abundant metal in the Earth's crust, and it is used in a surprisingly wide variety of products, such as cookware, aluminum foil, antacids, buffered aspirins, and some vaccines. Aluminum is even added to salt itself as an anticaking agent. Utility districts, in addition to adding Sodium Fluoride to the drinking water, also add aluminum.

These different exposures can cause aluminum poisoning, and let's not forget about Aluminum Chlorohydrate, which is used in anti-perspirant deodorants. Aluminum poisoning also comes from eating foods utilizing baking powder, such as Sodium Aluminum Phosphate, and Calcium Aluminum Phosphate! As a result, biscuits, pancakes, and waffles are excellent sources of aluminum. Read the ingredients on pancake mixes before buying them. Most of them are very faithful users of Sodium Aluminum Phosphate, instead of Monocalcium Phosphate. Please be aware that there are, thankfully, some brands with more natural ingredients and most importantly without aluminum!

Sodium Aluminium Phosphate is listed in *The New Additive Code Breaker*, a guidebook used in Australia and New Zealand and written in England by Maurice Hanssen and Jill Marsden. It states:

"Sodium aluminium phosphate has been considered by the toxicological committees on the basis of its aluminium rather than its phosphate component. Aluminium poses a problem because of the evidence that an accumulation of it in the cells of the nervous system could be potentially toxic, and responsible for Parkinson-type diseases and senile dementia."

Sodium Aluminium Phosphate is not permitted in foods in the countries of Australia and New Zealand.

(In British Commonwealth countries, aluminum is spelled aluminium.)

There are other toxic heavy metals that cause health problems. Among them are Arsenic (As), Antimony (Sb), Cadmium (Cd), Thallium (Tl), and even Copper (Cu) and Nickel (Ni). For further reading, please refer to an excellent article that came out in the May-June issue of *Autism Asperger's Digest Magazine*. There is also plenty of other literature about heavy metals, including Internet web sites.

A few years ago, while writing my 3rd science fiction novel: *Heritage Findings from Atlantis*, I decided to write some comments about lead in particular, from the perspective of the residents of the city of Zantaayer on a planet around the star Al Nitak. Below is the excerpt.

*　　*　　*

". . . scandal is only a moderate one compared to others."

"Such as what?" Fraxino asked.

"Such as nuclear power production and the high risk and dangers from that, not to mention possible harmful radiation exposure . . . and the element lead being added to Earth's fossil fuels for driving their automobiles and other vehicles . . . atrocious, that is. I tell you!"

"At least here on our world, we have hydrogen," said Rinto.

"And we can count our blessings on that one, sons," Glecko stated. "Earth's fuel companies *know* we can! Lead is extremely bad for living beings and is known for dulling intelligence, in addition to promoting chronic diseases because it accumulates within the body's tissues. It's a toxin which has no business *ever* being put into automobile fuels!"

"That really is appalling!" Tecoloteh declared. "We had no idea Earth's people would do anything so ridiculous!"

"They do," Rinto told Latorna and Tecoloteh.

"Special interest groups and other factions control a lot of Earth's scandals," Glecko went on, "and don't forget to consider that other star systems may be behind some of it, using Earth's people as test subjects for long term studies. Design your project crystals accordingly, and we'll make this galaxy a better place to live after all."

"Right on, Dad!" Fraxino declared.

"Dad, with the way we grow those crystals," said Rinto, "we'll have every one of those scandals squelched and abolished!"

"That's your intelligent genius at work, sons," their father commended them. "With your two friends from Atlantis, I'm sure you'll do fine work."

They continued talking and soon finished breakfast.

*   *   *

Even though some of what I wrote is speculation, it does make a statement and gets the message across to my readers the absurdity of the use of lead here on our world Earth!

Food Additives

In addition to heavy metals, there are many food additives that are bad for you, and the FDA faithfully allows free reign to food manufacturers to put them in food products to their heart's content! Around 90% of all cereals have BHT: Butylated Hydroxytoluene, a seriously bad food additive and preservative known to cause sterility in lab animals!

Referring to *The New Additive Code Breaker*, BHT does not occur in nature and is derived synthetically from p-cresol and isobutylene. It was developed initially around 1947 as an antioxidant for use with petroleum and rubber products.

BHA: Butylated Hydroxyanisole, is another nasty chemical used mostly for preserving cooking oils. It also doesn't occur in nature, and it is derived from a mixture of 2- and 3-tert-butyl-4-methoxy-phenol, prepared from p-methoxyphenol and isobutene.

In a food additive book called *Eater's Digest*, it states that BHA and BHT "should be barred from food; safe alternatives are available."

TBHQ: tert-Butylhydroquinone has a worse report. It is derived from petroleum. Small amounts of TBHQ have caused vomiting, nausea, ringing in the ears, delirium, suffocating feelings, and collapse! TBHQ is used as a preservative in certain foods, such as pies, some types of crackers, and even some types of loaf bread!

MSG: Monosodium Glutamate is very bad indeed, with many people having severe adverse allergic reactions to foods that contain it. Among them are numbness in the neck, hands, and chest, tightness in the jaw, vice like headaches, and temporary paralysis. In laboratory animals, MSG has caused damage to brain cells. Some food companies are "ashamed" that they put MSG in their foods, so they hide the fact that they put it in, by calling it other names such as "Hydrolyzed Vegetable Protein," "Autolyzed Yeast," and "Natural Flavoring."

For further reading about food additives, check various food additive codebooks and handbooks.

As far as foods are concerned, read the ingredients on all food labels, and just because it's clear of preservatives does not guarantee that it will *still* be clear the next year. Companies are bad about slipping additives in without your realizing it. Be consistent about continually checking food labels and ingredients.

I also recommend buying organically grown foods and 100% natural foods whenever possible.

Basically, closely monitoring food intake in the right proportions can really help a person achieve a closer sense of stability.

Breads are very bad about having food additives and preservatives such as Calcium Propionate, TBHQ, and lots of dough conditioners and emulsifiers such as Ethoxylated Mono-and di-glycerides and Sodium Stearoyl-lactylate, Potassium Bromate, and more still. Some of these cause migraine headaches and tightness in the chest, anxiety, and other reactions!

Nearly all soft drinks have 1/1000 (0.1%) Sodium Benzoate, another preservative and headache causer, not to mention beer and wine containing that and/or Sodium Bisulfite, which certainly contribute to hangovers . . . not just the alcohol!

People think I'm crazy and that I'm from Mars because I'm always so aware of foods, and I've been a stickler for reading ingredients in foods ever since I was age 10. If everyone were like me, food additive manufacturers would soon be out of business, and what a great day that would be for all of us! Why don't they send their products and byproducts of production to toxic waste dumpsites, or better yet send them to the Sun, instead of slipping them in our foods!

I have here included another excerpt from my 3rd novel: *Heritage Findings from Atlantis*. This one is about BHT.

*   *   *

Morning arrived with nice weather and clear blue-green skies. All of them got up and went into the kitchen where Glecko and Sosta fed them breakfast. There were various cereals and fruits.

"Here's a new one for you, guys," Glecko announced as he showed them a new box of cereal. *"Kellogg's* Bran Flakes Esperaña." He set the box of cereal on the table. "I just brought it home from the supermarket last night."

"You have *Kellogg's* cereals on Artenia, too?" Robert asked, somewhat surprised.

"We do now, as of this week," Glecko answered.

"Huh!" Steven commented and he laughed. "Earth's companies are having all kinds of influences here on this world. It's coming in from all different angles."

"Looks like *Kellogg's* has now expanded to a galactic level, too," Andrew remarked, laughing.

"Dad, how can they be able to sell this in Earth's alphabet?" Rinto wanted to know.

"I know. How can they get away with this?" Fraxino complained. "Why aren't they forced to conform to Artenia's standards and print the name in Artenian script? After all, very few Artenians know English."

"Kellogg's Bran Flakes Esperaña," said Rinto, shaking his head. "Totally Earth's alphabet."

"Look at that," Fraxino commented. "It even goes on to boast how it has Pyridoxine: for better hearing and mental acuity, and it's written in English. What's this world coming to?"

"I'm sure *Kellogg's* will soon get the message," Glecko told everyone reassuringly. "Since it's a new product by a new galactic company here on Artenia, I suspect they wanted to introduce it in the alphabet and language of its place of origin."

"I'll bet they're exporting it directly from *Kellogg's* on Earth," Chispo suggested, "until they can set up manufacturing of it, here on Artenia."

Steven was the first one to the box. He opened it and poured a bowl for himself. He began to munch on the flakes of cereal. "It tastes good enough . . . looks very much like Bran Flakes on Earth. I'll have to take a couple of boxes home to my dad. He's suffering from a little bit of hearing loss."

"Sorry to hear that," said Chispo.

"Maybe this Bran Flakes Esperaña will do the trick," Chris said reassuringly to Steven.

"Thanks."

Robert looked at the box of cereal some more. He read the nutrition information. "Good! It doesn't have any BHT in it."

"That's right," Glecko proudly stated.

"You mean you already knew that?" Robert asked. "It's all over our cereals back on Earth."

"I know it is," Glecko admitted. "You see, that's one of Earth's scandals . . . has to do with a government coverup scheme and cancer study. BHT, or by its real name: Butylated Hydroxytoluene, is a poisonous and dangerous byproduct of modern plastics production which began in the late 1940's on your world Earth. They had to figure out how to get rid of the chemical, and it dawned on them that preserving food was the answer, all under contract and agreement with top secret Earth government officials and cancer societies around the world. It's a nasty preservative which is strictly prohibited here on our world of Artenia, and *Kellogg's knows* it!"

"Golly!!" Robert declared, somewhat shocked.

"Glecko, how can you be sure of that?" Steven asked Glecko, doubting.

"I used to teach chemistry," he answered, "and I know about that chemical. Here on our world, it's a strict mandate that all hazardous chemicals and byproducts be sent *straight* to Al Nitak, which is by far, a *superior* incinerator to anything we could have on this world."

"Now that's smart thinking," Robert complimented. "Why can't they do that on our world, also?"

"Scandals, corruption, and undercover cancer studies," Glecko simply replied, his arms crossed.

"So," Chispo proposed, "what do we all want to do today?"

"There's a really neat back road that runs the ridge of the Ciruclar Mountains," Fraxino informed them. "It passes right by the scene where they found that crate and sacred story stone . . ."

*   *   *

As a disclaimer, of course we all know that *Kellogg's* has *not* expanded to a galactic level, nor do they know it, pertaining to BHT and it's being a "nasty preservative which is strictly prohibited here on our world of Artenia," nor that there exist such certain "Scandals, corruption, and undercover cancer studies," as Glecko simply replied with his arms crossed. Plus, *Kellogg's* Bran Flakes Esperaña is a fictitious cereal.

Any person or author has liberty of expression, of which I made use in my

3rd novel. I included that conversation about BHT, from the viewpoint of some residents of the city of Zantaayer, to make a statement and get the message to my readers pertaining to the absurdity of the continued and diligent use of BHT in almost all varieties of not only *Kellogg's* cereals, but many other major name brand cereals, also! I myself certainly agree with *Eater's Digest* that BHT should be barred from all foods.

I have also pulled another excerpt from my 3rd novel. This one is about MSG in particular.

*   *   *

"We've got more crystal arrays still up in the cave," Fraxino explained.

"Tomarius and his crew will have them teleported there," Rinto added. "We're leaving here shortly to have that arranged."

"Excellent work, sons," their father complimented. "Were your Atlantean friends of help?"

"Oh yeah," Rinto answered. "They've got a better handle on this than we do."

"Really?" Glecko asked with surprise.

"They really are whizzes when it comes to growing crystals," Fraxino stated.

"Well, I suppose that would make sense," Glecko admitted. "After all, they are original Atlanteans, who certainly know the art."

After looking over the array, they walked back in the house again. They ate some breakfast. Glecko started reading Zantaayer's morning newspaper.

"Land sakes! Another scandal from planet Earth!" he declared.

"What's it about this time?" Rinto asked his father.

"This report has to do with Earth's use of MSG, known as Monosodium Glutamate, another byproduct of manufacturing. Instead of disposing of it properly by sending it to the Sun, food and drug companies across planet Earth have been paid under the table to approve the nasty chemical to enhance food flavor, to the point that they don't even list it on the ingredients of food products that contain it."

"How can they get away with that?" Fraxino wanted to know.

"They use clever cover-up names like: Natural Flavoring, Autolyzed Yeast, and Hydrolyzed Vegetable Protein, of which MSG is a considerable part of each one of those."

"Dad, how scandalous do they get, down there on planet Earth?!" Rinto declared.

"I'm telling you!" Glecko agreed. "The report goes on to say that the use of MSG is at an all-time high, as a result."

"How awful!" Fraxino exclaimed.

"The main driving force behind it is intelligence suppression. MSG is a nasty chemical and has no business ever being added to food products. It causes headaches, and for those more allergic to it, it causes paralysis for up to hours and disarms certain people of their senses and mental capacity."

"Golly! Why don't they ban the stupid chemical?" Fraxino asked his father.

"Because chief administrations have been paid under the table," Glecko simply stated. "It's just one more part of the intelligence suppression study driven by unscrupulous factions that need to be halted. Let's just hope the arrays you four have built and grown do the trick."

"Thanks, Dad. We'll hope for the best," said Rinto.

"Of course, here on our world, as you know," Glecko pointed out, "nasty chemical byproducts like MSG are flown *straight* to Al Nitak, a far superior incinerator than what this world has to offer."

"Right on, Dad!" said Fraxino.

"And why can't Earth capture that bright idea?" Rinto asked his father.

"I wish they would, sons."

*   *   *

Some of what I wrote about MSG is likely speculation, but it is true that for many people, it causes headaches, and for those more allergic to it, it causes paralysis for up to hours and disarms certain people of their senses and mental capacity. On a TV report/interview several years ago, I saw some people interviewed who complained of suffering from those symptoms. The same news story documentary also said that the use of MSG in food is at an all-time high! Personally I think MSG has no place in human foods, and it should be banned entirely, considering the severe adverse reactions it causes in many people.

The *Kellogg's* Cereals Letter and BHT

Back in 1990, I collected a bunch of cereal boxes from *Kellogg's* of Australia, and I sent them home. Cereals there do not have BHT in them. I wrote *Kellogg's* of Michigan a detailed letter expressing my disapproval of their continued incessant use of BHT in 90% of their cereal brands, and I sent Xerox copies of literature from food additive codebooks, and the flattened cereal boxes. They didn't write me back, and when I called to follow up, they claimed they never received my package. I've always suspected that yes, they got the package, but slipped it in "file 13" because it must have struck a wrong chord with them. I'll bet they thought I was a nut case to have gone to all the trouble I did. Well, I insisted on a reply, and I sent Xerox copies that I had previously made of the cereal boxes along with a copy of the original letter. This time I got a reply.

Cereals are dry, packaged well, and have a long shelf life. Why do they put BHT in nearly all of them?! Why just 90%? Why not go all out and put BHT in 100% of them? Is there a clause or under-the-table regulation that states that 10% of the cereals have to be free of preservatives? It makes a person wonder, seeing that Australia does not use BHT in cereals at all. No one has successfully brought BHT to a halt. I even personally gave my U.S. senator extra cereal boxes from Australia with an explanatory letter, and not even he could get the BHT stopped. I gave it my best, to no avail, and I feel like I was placed on a list of psychotics because any further correspondence I have attempted with cereal companies has never been taken seriously.

One can see that when I am straightforward and prepare my case very well, it is not appreciated. In fact, it is resented! In that letter to Kellogg's, I told them the truth and was so straightforward with them that they probably felt like choking!

Some years later, I wrote *Kellogg's* a letter pertaining to the *Kellogg's* Nutri-Grain cereals. It was concerning why they started adding sugar to those types of cereals that always carried the motto and tradition of "No Sugar Added." I got no reply. So, I had some friends of mine write *Kellogg's* about the same subject and concern. Kellogg's wrote them nice, friendly reply letters of explanation. I got nothing of the kind, not even a reply! At least one friend mailed me the reply letter he received, and I have that.

Even though I may be an autistic Asperger's, they should have answered my letter, too.

I'm not psychotic, and I attempted to go after the "BHT monster" to get it stopped. I feel like the government has secret cancer studies going on behind our backs, which they don't have the right to do, but via the FDA's free reign approval, they continue to get away with it.

What's more? *Kellogg's* of Mexico only *recently* began adding BHT to their cereals, late 1999, and there it is 100%. All *Kellogg's* cereals varieties there have it! I was quite disappointed because I used to buy *Kellogg's* Corn Flakes and bring two or three boxes home after each stay in Mexico. I just want to know something. What took *Kellogg's* of Mexico so long to catch up to "modern" times?

Here's the difference between me and the rest of the general public. When I tell friends, relatives, or other people about BHT in cereals, most of them hardly bat an eye. Others show concern and even make a point to buy only cereals without BHT . . . but only for a while. They soon forget and revert to buying all types of cereals again, with the excuse that they only eat those cereals every now and then. Well, I don't revert, never! Cereals with BHT don't come into my home, and I don't eat them elsewhere either . . . Never!

What I don't understand is, why do other people, though very intelligent with some of them being engineers and doctors, all of them with rare exception (one case in Portland, Oregon) have BHT laden cereals in their homes?! This has been my observation through life, pertaining to cereals, and hardly anyone is ever going to speak up.

*   *   *

Robert Sanders, June 2001

APPENDIX

This section contains somewhat controversial topics and insights, that is, topics that didn't fit in very well with the mostly chronological flow of this book. They are here for the reader to enjoy, and most of this is my viewpoint about certain things, how they are and how they work.

Brain Development After Birth

Like I earlier stated, I would say that in my case of overcoming my autistic traits, I learned step by step, detail by detail (what others seem to know almost by instinct) the mannerisms of how to be a person and how to grow up during childhood.

Brain development is an important issue concerning autism. The neurons that send and receive sensory information are called *dendrites*, which are arranged inside the brain in a formation analogous to the branches of a tree. Therefore, the neurological setup of the brain can be called a *brain tree*. One could say that autistics have an underdeveloped brain tree and therefore don't always comprehend as well as normal people with fully developed brain trees.

Now who's to say that these brain trees can't go on and develope even after birth, that is, in childhood and even in adulthood, for that matter? I think the brain tree can evolve and transform into a fully developed one, and I believe that is what happened to me. Anyone who puts himself in the right mindset and frame of reference can overcome barriers and be an achiever.

I believe the brain is but a central processor of thoughts while most of the thinking or at least some of it occurs outside the body in the surrounding atmosphere. That means that even though a person might be lacking some of his/her brain, he/she can still think as well as a person with a fully developed brain. Plus, I believe in telepathy, which involves thoughts clearly *outside* the brain.

In a book called *The Holographic Universe*, by Michael Talbot, it is mentioned how patients who have had portions of their brains removed, for medical reasons, have never suffered the loss of specific memories. Memories are not stored in specific parts of the brain but instead are distributed throughout. There's still a lot we don't know about how a brain really works, or about how much thought process really takes place *within* that organ.

Thoughts Outside the Brain

To state one example from early childhood, when I was age 5, I had a strange experience of being pulled out of my body and being forcefully dragged feet first into the hall, where I heard some strange musical notes. I ran back to my bed, somewhat in fear. Perhaps it was a dream, but it seemed too real for that. So, yes, I believe in a detachable spirit with its own intelligence for each human alive on Earth, which leads me to the concept of thoughts outside the brain.

I believe in telepathy, despite the fact that a lot of Ph.D. clinicians and diagnosticians do not. I know this is a topic that a lot of people turn their backs to and ignore, but for the purposes of research, this topic needs to be seriously studied. As to the phenomenon of thoughts outside the brain. I've known what other people were thinking or doing in real life, though remote, through my intuition and also my dreams at times. On occasion, when drifting off to sleep, I've heard voices talk to me, and even tell me unique words.

Even feelings are, in a sense, thoughts outside the brain, and they are a form of telepathy.

As far as I'm concerned, while most people think all memories are stored inside the brain, most memories are actually stored outside the brain and body in the surrounding atmosphere, that is, in the ethereal energy field of each individual person, while very little of it is in the brain, which is merely a central processor of thoughts, a communication connector center for associating and recognizing the memories as they are thought and processed. Many memories are stored at physical locations, and when a person visits the same place again later in his or her life, he or she can remember more exact details of the place and can even remember what he or she was thinking about the last time he or she had been there.

All thoughts that a person thinks are literally recorded telepathically within the energy matrix of matter, that is, the material items of any location, such as rocks, soil, minerals, crystals, trees, or even buildings. The information of the thoughts are stored there indefinitely until the person returns to that site and triggers the appropriate recorded memories and thoughts to come forth and run through the mind of the visitor.

After all, one can realize that matter is mostly empty space, that is, bound up energy, and since it is mostly holographic in nature, there is literally a phenomenal amount of storage capacity within the energy matrix of matter itself of any location, and it can be tapped into later.

Reincarnation? Inexperienced Souls?

I repeat here what I stated early in this book that during my early childhood I felt really alien to the culture here, like maybe I was from a faraway star system. For those who believe in reincarnation, maybe this is my very first lifetime on Earth, while other humans alive here today may be living their 10th, 100th, or even higher number lifetime. They've had plenty of experience, but then since I'm on my first Earth human lifetime, I've had no experience. Therefore, I behaved very strangely in early childhood but finally got the hang of it by age 9 or 10 and became at least somewhat more normal.

In other words, I would say that in my case of overcoming my autistic traits, I learned step by step, detail by detail (what others seem to know almost by instinct) the mannerisms of how to be a person, and how to grow up during childhood, that is, how to live my life here on planet Earth.

At present, autism in humans is on the uprise, with a higher number per capita than ever before. This could be due simply to better testing and awareness, but it could also be due to inexperienced souls.

All of us are aware that there are more people on the planet than there ever have been before, and it will increase in population to a, no doubt, crowded future, if it isn't curbed. Each person has a lifeforce or spirit, also called a soul, that animates his/her body. Now in the past, there has been a ready supply of souls for what was a more stable population on Earth, but with the recent population explosion during the past very few generations, where have all the extra souls been coming from? Granted, many of them can be considered to have come from past lives here on Earth, meaning that the people with those souls have some experience. Well, what about all the extra people alive today? I believe their lifeforces or souls are likely from somewhere else, some of them reincarnated from alien lifeforms, some more intelligent and some less intelligent. Some may be from humans that lived elsewhere in other star systems in the galaxy, and some may be from other lifeforms altogether. What these have in common is that they have no prior Earth experience. They have a unique way of thinking, and they will likely have a more difficult time becoming adjusted to life here in this world and culture. In other words, they have to adapt and learn. Some will do it successfully, and others won't, the ones who are institutionalized.

To add to the concept of brain development and growth after birth, my speculation is that these alien souls or spiritual beings from elsewhere sometimes cause the brain and body to react differently and grow differently, that is, in different proportions than what is normal. It's like a lifeforce that is not quite properly aligned or synchronized with the Earth human blueprint design, and this can result in interfering with the normal human growth pattern for those people on this planet with alien souls.

I have talked with some of my past teachers, and some of them have told me how some of the teenagers in this day and time are just not as lively and are just not with it, more now than in the past, like 20 or 30 years ago. Some of my teachers were quite concerned about it. I actually explained to one of my teachers my theory of alien souls for some of those teenagers, and he was quite intrigued. He said I might be right.

I state the above speculation to point out that there is a lot out there that we humans don't know. While my reasons for my abnormalities in early childhood likely stemmed from autism, perhaps they also stemmed from living my first? life on Earth, one or both.

Negative Entities?

There are some people who think the more extreme causes of autism, or shall we say, severe autism, are caused by other-level entities, negative entities, bad energy systems, or what some would call "demon possession". This is especially believed in third world countries, but scientists who have trained in their fields of studies, more recently know that it's autism, caused by brain disorders, whether chemically imbalanced or genetic. Are they totally sure?

Well, I've read some of those reports and while most of the cases are genuine autism, let's not declare it right across the board 100%. I'm inclined to think a small percentage of those cases are caused by demon possession, or that is, negative entities. Now, why would I even begin to believe an archaic wild belief system like that? I'll tell you why.

(Before I go on further with this particular topic, I don't have a prestigious academic position that would be put at risk by some of my declarations in this book. Most people who write books pertaining to autism are degreed Ph.D.'s who would be committing academic suicide by stating what I'm stating in this topic. However, since I'm a self-employed individual, I am free to opinionate.)

I also want to comment and explain that everyone who is alive, since they have a lifeforce that keeps them animated, is unique in that they have different abilities and talents, and different mannerisms. That is because they have different programs by which they operate. Most computers are different in that they have different programs, and in a sense, all of us are walking computers.

Humans are somewhat analogous to computers, in that they have different programs or abilities and talents. These programs are energy systems with a life of their own, and they run under their own energy. Some of them stay with a person through his/her whole life, and others attach and/or detach at different time intervals.

These energy systems are considered by some to be spirits, guardian angels, demons, negative entities, other-level entities, etc. In a sense, they give us inspiration, abilities, and talents. Some of them are bad, like a virus or demon, and some of them are good, like a guardian angel. Others are in between, not doing any harm nor doing any good. For those who don't believe in demons, spirits, or entities, they can believe in programs. To me they are all one in the same, and the bottom line is that these *programs* define a person's character.

In 1999, I went to visit a group home one evening where several autistics, all of them more severe than I, lived and had meetings also. Several adults ran the "facility." Most of the autistics were teenagers, and they had the strangest behavior, but that was due to autism. However, there was one girl around age 17 who came into the room grunting and groaning, and she would give out sudden shrieks of horror always followed by a rash of vulgarities! She would scream without warning, and it got me angry, as sudden loud sounds annoy me. I yelled back at her and put my earplugs in.

She obviously didn't like my being there, and while I was trying to talk to the others, the girl shrieked and screamed several more obscenities and glared at me! I told the adults to get her out of there, and they took her to a back room where I continued to hear more horrifying shrieks and screams as they tried to calm her down.

I asked the adults how much she cussed, and her mother, who was at the meeting, said, "All the time. That's all she ever says." As far as I'm concerned, what more proof did I need? I think that girl was severely possessed, or severely altered by bad programs, but since her parents and other Ph.D. diagnosticians steadfastly think it's autism, they have decided to tolerate and live with a continuing nightmare! That is a misdiagnosis, in my opinion. Yes, autistics are known to throw tantrums, as an outlet to vent their frustrations, but their vocabulary is not a diligent list of vulgarities and obscenities.

The main point of this topic is that people must keep an open mind and consider all possibilities when diagnosing people for autism. Each person is a different and unique case. We must not throw them all in the same basket. We must not turn deaf ears and turn our backs to considering the possibility of demon possession, saying that's just malarkey that third world nations believe.

There are exceptions, as the above example shows.

Now it could be that I'm totally wrong about my diagnosis of the shrieking horror girl. Perhaps she really is severely afflicted with autism, that or her brain is a wired nightmare, or there might be more alien reasons for her personality than I have ever imagined. Enough on my speculation. Experts can scratch their heads to try and find the final correct answer on that one.

As I earlier stated, all of us in a sense are walking computers. One can speculate some more about demons, other-level entities, negative entities, or bad energy systems. They are somewhat analogous to computer programs (viruses) with lives of their own, and associated with each person involved, they are capable of bringing about discouraging phenomena, such as what occurred to me in my topic, *Derailed Good Intentions*. I'm not sure about it myself, and I know a lot of people don't believe in the existence of "entities," but in attempts to explain the reality of what occurred in *Derailed Good Intentions*, and in recognition to those *telepathic forewarnings* that it seems like some of my friends received, including *dreams* that scared them off, I must attribute my speculation to those types of "culprits" as being responsible for sending them false messages about me. Now it could be that I have lack of understanding of the whole concept and that there could be other much more alien reasons for the phenomena.

Demons and negative entities can be thought of as being synonyms for the words evil and error, which are false concepts of reality and, as far as I'm concerned, do not belong in our society.

Coincidences in General

In my life, I have experienced several coincidences. Another name for coincidence is synchronicity. I haven't experienced very many coincidences, but some of them are remarkable. I mention the topic in this book not knowing for sure if it has anything to do with being an Asperger's. There are some people who say there is no such thing as a coincidence. All coincidences are predestined, and there are no accidents. Others say that there are accidents. I say that coincidences are caused from higher levels of existence. I have lifted an excerpt from my 2nd science fiction novel: *Mission Beyond the Ice Cave: Atlantis-Mexico-Zotola*, where I explain my thoughts and viewpoints about coincidences. Below is the excerpt.

*   *   *

"While it is a known fact that some of the past ancient human civilizations arrived to Earth by teleporting themselves from their world existing in alternate realities, it has been theorized that destiny originates from higher levels of thought in alternate realities. Quite often, humans have dreams, and though they don't always realize it, they are actually visiting those alternate realities in their mind and spirit, sometimes so clearly that they feel like they've actually been there. In truth, some of those alternate realities are where their long ago ancestors came from.

"In the true sense of reality, there are multiple levels of consciousness, and some of the higher levels are mentally out of reach or out of range. At these higher levels of thought in alternate realities, there are minds which operate and think and cause us on this level to experience coincidences and various synchronicities which cause us to think many actions are predetermined or destined. Through the complex system of multiple levels of consciousness, there is truth to this. As those beings at higher levels of reality plan their lives and thoughts, we at lower levels are sometimes affected by their actions."

"Huh! That's really interesting," Steven remarked. "So, what is actually going on are higher levels of thought, and since they know more than we do, they therefore cause our destiny to occur on this level."

"Exactly," Fraxino agreed. "In truth, when you really look at all the levels, there is no destiny. Each being on whatever level plans his life and causes his own destiny as a result."

"I don't know," said Rinto. "I believe in destiny. I mean, we are affected by higher levels of thought and by their plans. By definition, that is destiny."

*   *   *

The Healing Power of the Mind

For many years I have believed that the power of the mind is capable of many things. More specifically, the mind may be referred to as the subconscious mind or divine mind. As I previously stated in the topic, *Brain Development After Birth*, anyone who puts himself in the right mindset and frame of reference can overcome barriers and be an achiever. Not only does this involve overcoming

Asperger's Syndrome, but this can and does also involve healing oneself of sickness and disease, even incurable diseases. Believing a disease is incurable is believing an erroneous concept. Many people think only material medicine heals a person, but the truth is that a person's mindset and lifeforce are what actually heal a person of sickness. The Greek philosopher Hippocrates stated, *"The natural healing force in each one of us is the greatest force in getting well."* After all, each one of us has a lifeforce or spirit that animates our physical bodies.

For example, when a person is cut or scraped, the wound heals itself, right? That is exactly what the healing force is and does, and while that sort of healing is small scale, the same kind of healing takes place on a larger scale for curing oneself of diseases and major illnesses.

Yes, medicine in some cases helps the healing along faster, but it is far from a cure of all diseases, because there are still so many diseases that are incurable, even in this new millennium.

But don't be discouraged. Even though doctors can't cure certain diseases through modern medicine, there are literally thousands of people on this planet that have been healed of various "incurable" diseases anyway. After all, if a person is capable of becoming ill with a disease, then a person is also capable of becoming well again. This may be viewed as a transformation back to the state of original wellness and self. There are some really good books with compilations of selected testimonials of "miraculous" healings. While researching for material to put in this book, I came across several books with documentaries, even notarized affidavits, that convinced me that it is no hoax.

Some people accuse me of not being reality based about my philosophy of diseases and curing them. The reason I'm "not reality based" is the fact remains that there are so many diseases that are still incurable with "modern" medicine, and I put the word *modern* is in quotes because doctors have just *not* been able to find a cure for everything. Yes, they have progressed remarkably in certain areas, but certainly not all.

I also mention that in the *New Testament* of the *Holy Bible*, it is common knowledge that Jesus of Nazareth walked the Earth and healed literally thousands of people of all kinds of diseases, many of them incurable. That healing energy he tapped into is still available today. It has always been available, in all parts of the universe. Just like radio frequencies are available to be tapped into for transmission of radio and TV signals, so is the healing energy available also.

How is this possible? Many people, especially doctors, will tell you they have studied enough biology and organic chemistry to understand diseases, how they work, and how to stop them, that is, through medicine. Well, the power of the mind is certainly strong enough to transcend organic chemistry, to transcend diseases, and *abolish* them.

For years I have thought of matter as being mostly empty space and made of pure energy. After all, atoms consist of a central nucleus of protons and neutrons with electrons whizzing around them *way* on out there from the nucleus, causing the volume each atom occupies to be mostly empty space. In other words, I believe matter is nothing more than material thought, and with the right mindset and know-how, it can be transformed. Matter and reality are much more pliable and transformable than most of us realize, and what most of see as miracles can actually be brought about.

I believe the wave of the future is that doctors are going to come to realize on a grander scale that what Hippocrates said is very true and is not to be scoffed. It's not so much the medicine that does the curing as it is the healing force within the body of each person. Proof of this is thoroughly discussed in *The Holographic Universe*. Many patients have been given placebos in place of the real medicines, and they have been cured anyway. I also highly recommend reading a very important book called *Spiritual Healing in a Scientific Age*, by Robert Peel.

Mind Is All One

In a sense, mind is all one. All levels, including the subconscious level, merge into one free landscape. I have lifted an excerpt out of my 3rd science fiction novel: *Heritage Findings from Atlantis*, to give the reader an idea.

*   *   *

Fraxino translated Morris' comment to the Atlanteans, who shook hands with Morris and wished him well.

"You'll be seeing me from time to time," Morris went on. "However, I do feel it is my duty to make you aware of something, as this might ease this project's timely completion. It's been my increasing feeling that the existence of the subconscious mind is a myth. It's a learned response which gives human beings the excuse of committing unacceptable actions, like the mass dumping of those precious crystals and artifacts. While there are higher levels of consciousness and higher level beings, the human mind can become unified and be consciously aware of different levels, in addition to merging the conscious and subconscious into one program. Let that movie be a lesson to you. Senseless actions would be far fewer if the humans would learn to do with their minds what I've just stated.

"With that said, I must leave you. All the best."

"Morris, what about . . .?" Rinto began to ask.

* * *

Mind is all one. It is a free landscape that is open and can be explored. It is not sectioned off, like many people have come to believe. That's just what human society has taught us through cultural influence and is what we have learned and taken for granted. The right mindset is all a matter of focus, awareness, and how we look at things. Granted there still is the subconscious "level" which is the most versatile and awake area of the mind. It may be considered like a broad beam of light, as it goes about picking up data and information and telepathically communicating with others outside of our conscious awareness. The important thing to realize is that not even the subconscious mind is sectioned off. We can merge the "sections" of our mind and be more aware of that subconscious mind of ours. For what human society has been taught, to think in certain ways, and that there are different levels or sections of the mind and consciousness, we have in essence been taught not to be natural explorers. Our mindset has been pigeonholed. We need to broaden our mindset and see it all. The conscious waking state may be considered like a beam of light focused on certain areas, compared to the broad beam of light of the subconscious. That conscious beam of light is capable of accessing and shining on the whole landscape, not just sections. Every frame of reference or mindset is flexible. It is not set in stone. We are capable of expanding our horizons, and we can add "programs" to our mindset, that is, change our own perspective to enable us to explore new ideas and concepts.

As stated earlier, it's all a matter of awareness. How well do we really understand our mental health? How adept are we about operating within our mindset? How adept are we in our abilities to create reality for ourselves, to achieve what we desire?

* * *

CONCLUSION

I believe I have successfully overcome being an Asperger's. I never considered myself as handicapped, which likely made the overcoming process a lot easier. Plus the reader has realized that I have made full use of my condition in many positive ways, having accomplished many projects in my life.

Like I stated at the beginning, I here reiterate that Asperger's are not to be loathed nor avoided, even though they might not have the best social skills and behavior. Most of them are good decent people with a lot to offer. Many of them are very thorough and exacting, and they have phenomenal memories. They are persistent and meticulous, which are advantageous for accomplishing tasks, plus other good traits. It has to do with a matter of focus in concentrating on projects at hand.

Asperger's find ways to expand their choices to make full use of their condition. They find a different way around something to get to the same point. As there is always more than one way to do something, it is not wrong to go about accomplishing something in a unique way. Sometimes it is the better way. Many Asperger's can see something that a lot of normal people cannot see, and as a result, they can improve a situation.

One example has to do with how I picked up that curved piece of Eucalyptus bark and handed it to the bus driver, so he could get water into the radiator. Another example has to do with the cattle troughs that Temple Grandin has ingeniously designed.

It's all a matter of how to cause the general public to look at the whole thing. People with Asperger's Syndrome deserve to be accepted and appreciated in society just like everyone else. They have their place in this world, and I give thanks to many of them for bringing into reality their inventions and creations, *most* of them with the goal of making this world a better place to live.

Again, I reiterate the importance that anyone who puts himself in the right mindset and frame of reference can overcome barriers and be an achiever. It is all a process as we explore new ideas and concepts.

Robert Sanders atop Mt. Whitney in California, September 1992

REFERENCES, BIBLIOGRAPHY, RELATED READING

The following listings refer to selected books, magazine articles, and newspaper articles that were brought to my attention. Of course, there are numerous other books and articles pertaining to autism and Asperger's Syndrome, and they can be found in libraries or through search engines of various web sites of the *Internet*.

Note: If any of the below books are out of print, there are plenty of used copies available and listed on http://www.abebooks.com

Alquzok, Robert, *Walking Between Worlds: a novel of an American in Mexico*, Armstrong Valley Publishing Company, Murfreesboro, Tennessee, 2001

Asperger, Hans and Uta Frith, *Autism and Asperger's Syndrome*, Cambridge University Press, Cambridge, England, 1991

Bashe, Patricia Romanowski and Barbara L. Kirby and Tony Attwood (Foreword), *The Oasis Guide to Asperger Syndrome: Advice, Support, Insight, and Inspiration*, Crown Publishers, New York, New York, 2001

Beers, Clifford Whittingham, *A Mind That Found Itself: an Autobiography*, Doubleday, New York, New York, 1953, first published in 1908

"Brain Chemicals May Point Toward Cause of Autism," *The Tennessean*, Nashville, Tennesseee, 4 May, 2000, Section A, page 8

Collins, Abby Ward and Sibley J. Collins, *Autism: Now What?*, Phat Art 4, Stratham, New Hampshire, 2002

Eddy, Mary Baker, *Science and Health with Key to the Scriptures*, The Christian Science Board of Directors, Boston, Massachusettes. 1875-1994

Extreme Health, *Oral Chelation and Age-Less Formula*, Alamo, California
Extreme Health, *Heavy Metal Toxicity*, Alamo, California
(For more information, see http://www.extremehealthus.com)

Grandin, Temple Ph.D., *Thinking in Pictures and Other Reports from My Life with Autism*, Doubleday, New York, New York, 1995

Hanssen, Maurice with Jill Marsden, *The New Additive Code Breaker*, Lothian Publishing Company Pty Ltd., Melbourne, Victoria, Australia, 1989

"Heavy Metals," *Autism Asperger's Digest Magazine*, Future Horizons, Inc, Arlington, Texas, May-June 2002, pages 12-18

Jacobsen, Michael F., *Eater's Digest, The Consumer's Factbook of Food Additives*, Doubleday Anchor Books, Garden City, New Jersey, 1972

Ledgin, Norm, comments by Temple Grandin, Ph.D., *Diagnosing Jefferson: Evidence of a Condition that Guided His Beliefs, Behavior, and Personal Associations*, Future Horizons, Inc., Arlington, Texas, 2000

Mindell, Earl, *Unsafe at Any Meal*, Warner Books, New York, New York, 1987

Murphy, Dr. Joseph, *The Power of Your Subconscious Mind*, Prentice Hall, Englewood Cliffs, New Jersey, 1963

"A Neurologist's Notebook: An Anthropologist on Mars," by Oliver Sacks, *The New Yorker Magazine*, New York, New York, 27 December, 1993, pages 106-125

"Number of Kids, Teens with Disabilities Rises," by D'Vera Cohn, *The Washington Post*; printed in *The Tennessean*, 6 July, 2002, section A, page 13

Peel, Robert, *Spiritual Healing in a Scientific Age*, Harper and Row Publishers, San Francisco, California, 1987
(This book is presently out of print. However, there are plenty of used copies available and listed on http://www.abebooks.com)

Rudee, Martine and Jonathan Blease, *Traveler's Guide to Healing Centers and Retreats in North America*, John Muir Publications, Santa Fe, New Mexico, 1989

Sacks, Oliver, *An Antropologist on Mars, Seven Paradoxical Tales*, Alfred A. Knopf, New York, New York, 1995

Sanders Jr., Robert S., *Mission of the Galactic Salesman*, book 1 of the Galactic Salesman trilogy, Armstrong Valley Publishing Company, imprint of Eggman Publishing Company, Nashville, Tennessee, 1996

Sanders Jr., Robert S., *Mission Beyond the Ice Cave: Atlantis-Mexico-Zotola*, book 2 of the Galactic Salesman trilogy, Armstrong Valley Publishing Company, Murfreesboro, Tennessee, 1999

Sanders Jr., Robert S., *Heritage Findings from Atlantis*, book 3 of the Galactic Salesman trilogy, Armstrong Valley Publishing Company, Murfreesboro, Tennessee, 2000

"The Secrets of Autism," *Time Magazine*, Time, Inc., New York, New York, 6 May, 2002, pages 46-56

Talbot, Michael, *The Holographic Universe*, Harper Collins Publishers, New York, New York, 1992

"Understanding Autism," (re: toxic metals, biochemical imbalances in the brain), by William Walsh, Pfeiffer Institute, *McNeil Lehrer News Hour*, PBS TV, 24 August, 2001

Willey, Liane Holliday, *Asperger Syndrome in the Family: Redefining Normal*, Taylor and Francis Publishers, 2001.

Printed in the United States
6317